FORMS OF TAXATION

Forms of Taxation

Lawrance George Lux

Writers Club Press
New York Lincoln Shanghai

Forms of Taxation

Writers Club Press
an imprint of iUniverse, Inc.

For information address:
iUniverse, Inc.
2021 Pine Lake Road, Suite 100
Lincoln, NE 68512
www.iuniverse.com

ISBN: 0-595-25795-X (pbk)
ISBN: 0-595-65340-5 (cloth)

Printed in the United States of America

Contents

Preface

One of the oldest Jokes of Mankind contemplates the inevitability of Death and Taxes. It is rhymed in almost every human society, and has been through much of these societies' histories. Leadership always desires payment for itself. It also desires funding for it's own pet projects, sustenance for their own personal expansion of power and support; through the use of public funds to enrich the Few, whose support is necessary for continuance in power. Many would claim this a sour view of Politics; but in it's study, one reaches the conclusion no public effort would ever be undergone, if such effort did not benefit some privileged segment of the body politic.

A case in point can be derived from the Advertising and Entertainment industries, during the period of the Second World War. Both Industries suffered from personnel shortages, increased supply materials costs, and constriction of shooting schedules and locations. They were intensely supervised by Government, to insure they conformed to the current propaganda effort of the Government; a process which caused an average delay of two months in the production schedule. Both industries showed consistent profits in excess of any seen before; all due to very rich Government subsidy. It can be shown these Profits would not have been present with the same level of production evident before the War. It can even be proven levels of production associated with the War would not have produced such Profits without Federal subsidy.

The Author means not to discriminate against these industries, who probably expressed as high a level of patriotism as shown by American industry during the War. They were precisely used because the two industries actually expressed the lowest markup of wholesale prices for their products as any in America during this Period, and still derived a greater enrichment through Government subsidy. Business personnel who rant against provision of Government supply, because of suggested low profitability; directly lie through their teeth. There is no more lucrative production in existence, especially in the United States.

One of the great angers of Taxpayers lay in the fact they get little market value of purchase with their tax dollars. Government siphons off the cost of Tax Collection, then payment of themselves; all such Wages consistently higher than private employment for equivalent labor. They then dispense the remainder of funds to sectors which generate the greater political support; mostly of benefit only to special interest groups outside the general polity. The Government again intervenes to award Contracts based upon the acquirement of additional political support, so the Contracts are slanted to raise Supplier profits higher than the norm of private business. The above operation cuts approximately sixty percent of the purchasing power of the Tax dollar. It does not appease the general Taxpayer when this loss of purchasing power provides enrichment to special interests; almost always possessing higher Income and Capital than they themselves; worsened by Tax Break privileges granted to the privileged classes.

The above is not a rant against the American system of Politics, for it stands as the modus operandi of all political systems; no matter how organized. The Privileged subsume control of political leadership, in order to better their already present advantage. Revolutionary regimes inevitably simply institute their own Privileged Class, simply changing the criteria of admission to the special class. There remains no way to forestall the progression of politics, which retains no difference from corruption itself. The degree of political corruption can be quantified by the longevity of the regime. We are not on a perfect World; one does not exist.

The evils of Tax Use stands in the realm of the Philosopher, not the Economist; both understand the hazards of taxation, but the Economist goes further. He understands the mode of taxation can bring additional duress to Taxpayers, through the simple manner of their implementation. The additional duress expresses itself as greater difficulty for the Taxpayer in the simple process of making a living. Taxes can destroy this ability, not just through simple theft of their property by Government; but in the manner this theft takes place.

The Author must here state he understands the process of Community Services provision, along with the payment of Infrastructure costs. A minimum level of Government stands as mandatory, else the economic process reverts to a tribal level of production. He would like to state for the Record, though, taxes continue at a minimum diversion theft, of at least a quarter of the total collected; maintaining a systematic enrichment of privileged classes, all of which is of little benefit to the general polity. Most will discount the above as Liberalism expressing animosity to business; it is not!. Tax Policy Economists continue as enlightened Conservatives, who see large Government budgets for what they are; payments to underwrite an aristocracy, one which is inherently destructive of economic opportunity for the common Citizen.

Government has advanced a great distance from Roman times, where the Senate let Tax Farmers bid on regions of the Republic, and later Empire. Whoever bid the most received control of the region, where he could extort what funds he could from the populace by any means; retaining control as long as he sent back to the Senate what funds he had promised. The tax rate depended upon how many Sword-wielders the Tax Farmer could hire. The after-tax income of the Populace became whatever they could effectively hide. It does and does not remind of the present operation.

This Work examines some of the past efforts of Governments to collect Taxes. It goes further to examine the economic effects specifically of the manner of collection, as well as the social ramifications. It continues to examine some of the current operational systems for collecting Taxes, and examines the effects of these efforts. It finishes with the presentation of certain theoretical tax systems, with estimates of their potential economic impact. The total will hopefully raise common understanding of the process of Taxation, it's resultant economic impact, and how certain elemental changes in the taxing systems could improve economic performance.

1

The Head Tax

The original Head Tax was loved by Rulers concerned only with the raising of funds to pay troops, and provide for their own personal comforts. It consisted of a financial charge for every person in the realm. Tax Collectors only had to count noses, then multiply this number by the rate of charge. The Ruler found ease in the setting of the Tax, requiring only knowledge of the number of subjects and the necessary amounts to be raised; he could simply adjust the rate to draw the specified, required revenue. The Tax Collectors found this Head Tax more disturbing, as the ease of collection did not match the ease of placement.

The first complication in Collection arose from the fact many of the noses counted were either very young, or very old. Extraction of the Tax from these elements was quite hard, as they generally had insufficient funds. Two methods could be adopted to counteract this tendency: the noses counted could be limited to certain Ages, or the Tax Collector could assign a Head of the Household; who would be responsible for payment for all in the Household. Both methods had advantages and disadvantages.

The Ruler disliked the first methods, because reduced numbers of noses counted; meant less total Revenue derived from Tax collection. A simple solution was simply to raise the financial charge rate. This again brought complications. His subjects tended to object to the tax assessment; Tax revolts having been recorded back through the Ages, beginning with the City-States of the Fertile Crescent around 8000 B.C. This condition could be controlled with sufficient troops; but they had to be paid, else Soldiers' revolts became a reality also extending as far back.

An excessively steep Tax rate also contained the seed of another economic hazard; such charges often exceeded the effective ability to pay of many subjects. They simply could not pay, if they did not make enough. Total Revenue again fell short, simply because no amount of battering would raise funds, where there were none to be raised. The Ruler generally came to agree with the Tax Collectors, who favored holding the Head of the Household responsible.

The 'Head of the Household' concept generated it's own set of preoccupations. Use of the Household allowed all productive members of the Household to contribute towards payment of the Tax. It also presented the possibility of the whole bill falling on the Head of the Household, especially; as the Head was arbitrarily designated by the Collector, and might not have the power to enjoin participation in payment. A counter-effect could also be noticed, as families united; Tax Collectors often the need to bring considerable force with them in their collection efforts. This incurred increase in troop complements, with added pay demands; all insisting on larger revenues being raised. The costs of Tax Collection had been established, magnifying as rates were raised.

The Head Tax possessed an additional Economic disadvantage, which Today is called Tax regression. Taxes are deemed to be Progressive, if ability to pay determines the rate to be assessed; those with more, pay more because they can. This attains importance in the examination of the Tax Burden upon Citizens. The prime incentive in setting a Tax rate need to be the proper apportion of Tax, so the same percentage of Income is paid by all Taxpayers. The amount of funds paid need increase as separate Incomes increase. The Head Tax does not carry this characteristic. Regressive tax, like the Head tax, make lower incomes pay equally with the more fortunate in income; traditionally, it distracts from the full participation of the lower income classes in the Economy.

Importance of equalization of Tax Burden remains much debated by Economists, though all agree a Head Tax contains too large a Tax regression. Inequality of Tax Burden means a sharp loss of Consumer Demand among lower incomes, under tax regressive conditions. Inequality of Tax Burden means failure to accumulate Capital, in overly-progressive tax conditions. Many Economic studies investigate the effects of tax progression and regression, none provide a definitive answer; but almost all Economists agree there is economic value in equalization of Tax Burden, far exceeding any moral imperative.

The case of the Head Tax regressiveness can be easily understood. Every doubling of Income over the lowest Income levels, allows for increase of Consumption or Capital accumulation fully equal to the full value of the Head Tax. The loss of Consumption by the lowest Income level is the difference between what they pay, and what they would pay if the Tax Burden was equalized. Actual difference can only be accurately estimated by a economic progression analysis, but this Author uses a quick estimate; the lowest Income levels lose eight percent of the Consumption value of the total Head Tax, for each level of Income which doubles the lowest Income. This equates to Incomes ten times the magnitude of the lowest Income costing a total loss of Consumption of the lowest Income class, of some eighty percent of the value of the Head Tax. Many would complain this number is excessive, but economic progression analysis expresses the lowest productive Incomes under a Head Tax; should be paying only about nine percent of what they do, with Tax Burden equalization.

The Head Tax, though, held an economic liability which provided doom to any such system. It proves most regressive to families. The simple birthing of Children multiplied the tax payment under the Head Tax. Those Households with the highest Support costs were made to pay the largest Tax assessment. This reduced the Support consumption of the Households, bringing many disadvantages.

Households were not provisioning properly the labor necessary for the Economy. Participating labor elements of the Household were not getting enough Food, Shelter, or rest. Non-participating elements of the Household were equally impoverished, with loss of future labor potential through malnourishment in personal growth stages. Attainment of labor skills suffered throughout the Household as consequence. Labor productivity declined in both the short, and the long run. Both Household and Government suffered under the lowered productivity of the economic performance. The Head tax may have slowed human development by as much as a Century.

The Head Tax did not last long when confronted with modern Economic conditions, but lasted far too long in the history of Mankind. The inherent tax regression of the assessments directly reduced the productivity, and retarded capitalization of the Economy. Government costs can be actually proven to have increased, due to this restriction. The Head Tax was the first example of Government taxation reducing the Standard of Living, while expanding itself in a malignant growth of Police power. It will not be the last expression of such Government operation.

2
The Salt Monopolies

Another ancient form of taxation was the Salt Monopolies. They are called such by Economists because Salt was the most common Necessity utilized in this manner. What the taxing Government instituted was a line monopoly on some commodity needed by all. Salt became the most prevalent, as it was the easiest to mine, load, and distribute with the use of Corvee labor (labor demanded by the Government upon the Locals, as additional form of tax). The Government used these line monopolies on Necessities to raise revenue in lieu of direct taxation.

The Revenue was assured for the Government, as Citizens would not evade payment for a commodity needed for life and well-being; unlike assessed Tax. These State line monopolies covered many commodities and economic activities; Postal services a modern-day reflection of the old line monopolies. The Russian Navy once controlled all freightage on the Black Sea, by way of sinking Competitors. The British Navy once controlled the importation of Opium into China, leading to eventual war. Rice was another commodity often co-opted by the controlling Governments throughout Asia; Food monopoly possessing bulk to limit smuggling.

Rice and Salt proved excellent for these monopolies, as Peasants could be taxed in either amount; as the quantities could be fractionalized to the appropriate degree, as to be a suitable replacement for money. Both could be produced through individual action by the Peasantry; with the populace suppliers sufficiently dispersed, product price-setting could be monopolized by the Government in both roles of Purchaser and Seller of product. Russia still maintains some vestiges of the Salt monopoly, while China still uses the Rice Tax in almost one-quarter of the Country. These State line monopolies are not an extinct species.

They have existed since the period of the Fertile Crescent, and undoubtedly pre-dated actual minting of money; making them the probable oldest form of taxation. The Chinese Rice Tax provided almost all Government revenues in China through the Imperial period, and probably still earns almost a third of Chinese Governmental revenues. Their longevity resides in the fact of Consumer inability to refuse purchase, even at State monopoly pricing. They have the added advantage of less necessary mintage of Coin and Currency. Government enjoys the benefit of provision of weights and measures, so revenues can be raised without noticeable public comment.

Citizenry relatively enjoyed such line monopolies, as they were conducted in commodities which they could understand; unlike the money evaluations, which required a minimum of counting skills and economic understanding. Most in the Age of Illiteracy could not understand the taxation, though the Peasants felt the Rice or Salt tax was exceedingly high. Their concern did not extend beyond their immediate needs; knowing Rice or Salt shortfalls in their personal households would not be replaced. The resale of these products in town and city produced the real revenue for the Government, but Peasants had no concept of the resale price in urban areas.

The economic impact of these State line monopolies find tough expression in the quantification analysis of Economic studies. Such monopolies undoubtedly allowed Governments to tax producer Peasants much higher than they would otherwise have accepted, due to the plentitude of the product involved. This may seem hard to visualize when considering Chinese famines, yet; Wealth was considered in terms of filled Bags of Rice, not in little pieces of metal or paper. The

Government taking two filled Bags, still left three filled Bags at home. It was hard for the Peasants to translate a filled Bag of Rice into the two Cups necessary per day. They did so in order to survive, but the concept of acquiring an additional Cup a day for Sale in large amounts after many days, was beyond them; or they were terrorized from such Sale by Government officials and soldiers.

The State monopolies demanded many pieces of expensive metal from the town folk, in order for them to obtain their two Cups of Rice per day. Urban populations probably paid three to four times the Food Cost they would have paid, under normal production conditions. Many wonder how ancient Rulers could amass such treasures, and build such exquisite temples and palaces. These State monopolies was the method of capital accumulation; leading ruling classes to possess almost ten thousand times the yearly income of the common laborer in these societies.

Most may think these State line monopolies were limited to a few limited Items in old feudal societies. China had in excess of a thousand such monopolies, as late as the turn of the Twentieth Century. Thailand still has over two hundred monopolies in place. Products included embrace Meat, Fish, Salt, Rice, Wheat, Barley, Corn, Hemp, Iron, Cooper, Pottery Clay, Timber and Wood, Rope, Canvas, Rice bags, wagon wheels, Carts, Cars, and Trucks. The List could be extended endlessly.

The most important areas of State monopoly were Food, wood for cooking and building, metal products, cooking utensils, fuel, and cloth. The ability of the Government to constrict economic activity, allowed it to become the real Monopoly of the respective Economies. This paramountcy was maintained by the ability to control Trade, so they operated in a closed economy; or one in which they set the prices of importation. Citizens under such State monopolies probably paid in excess of one-third of their yearly income as State revenue.

The economic consequence of these monopolies assures product pricing above normal production costing, directly reduced productivity, profits, and Wages. Un-monopolized products rose as a result, by at least half of their normal production cost. Labor and Management received less real-value payment for their production, because of monopoly-set pricing of products which they needed. Every Sector suffered from excessive Resource pricing, higher production costs, lower profit margins, and lessened Sales.

The regressive nature of the State line monopolies is easily established, with the lower Incomes paying at the same rate, or higher rate, than the wealthy, privileged classes. The aforementioned higher rate came from Peasant restriction from purchase in Retail outlets of the Privileged. Colonials did not start the practice of excluding Commoners from restaurants and stores. The practice of licensing of business had been quickly adopted in ancient society, as far back as the Roman Republic, ancient Judea, and Athens of famed democracy; so the poor of those societies could not rise, or even obtain part-time added labor.

There remains some historical speculation the old feudal Guilds originally started as State line monopolies, where the Controllers of the monopoly restricted employment in the industry. Normal production activity finds no way to implement such Guilds. This may not seem of great moment to Historian or Economist, but it is speculated these Guilds (present to some degree in all feudal societies) actually forestalled the Industrial Revolution by almost three hundred years; all due to the restrictive employment practices.

3

Tariffs and Imposts

Tariffs consist solely of Government tax upon the importation of products; imposts are government tax upon goods transferred through a governmental region. Free Trade advocates call for the elimination of Tariffs, while Protectionists call for Tariff maintenance. Almost no one discusses imposts, though they still exist in the form of Lodging taxes, fuel transfer taxes, and Port docking and unloading fee taxes. Any and all of the like taxes can be considered Transportation taxes, though there are Transportation taxes which are not tariffs or imposts.

Traditional Economic theory on tariffs stipulate their implantation protects domestic production, so domestic capitalization rises with the added protection; though domestic Consumers are left with higher product prices. Revisionist Economic theory suggests tariffs do not alter Consumer Demand for imported goods over the long-run: their argument says the tariffs reduces the demand for foreign currencies in the tariff nation, raising the value of the tariff nation currency, so imported goods become cheaper even with the tariff. All are agreed, though, tariffs increase the cost of Goods to domestic Consumers; thereby reducing Consumer Demand for those Goods.

Both Economic arguments ignore the most vital element in both tariffs and imposts. Each tax reduces the profitability of location production, through increase of the costs of Transportation. Profitability of location production occurs through proximity to production materials and/or shipping in the form of Product which is most Cost-effective. Tariffs can make domestic production cost-effective, by elimination of the savings in shipping costs by foreign production, channeling to a form cheapest shipped—domestic production. A counter-argument can also be made, if bulk shipment of raw materials stands as cheaper than the finished Product; which cancels the effect of location production profitability; Tariffs bring raised domestic employment.

Tariffs sometimes nullifies the impact of costs of production, where fuel, labor, or capital equipment is higher in domestic production. Tariffs, in this case, do not actually increase the cost of domestic purchase; the added value of domestic production more than makes up for the increases in purchase pricing. Tariffs provide for added domestic economic performance, with normal production profits off this production. The Protectionist argument gains weight against the Free Trade argument, due to the fact of domestic standard of living increase, under conditions of increases in domestic consumption due to native production.

A most important element in the Tariff argument consists in the nature of the tax distribution of domestic versus foreign production. Domestic production has paid the normal tax assessment in the production process, which is associated with the locale of production. Foreign production has paid the same series of tax assessment, but not to the government of the importing nation. This net loss must be assessed, when considering the added cost to the Consumer of a tariff on imported products. The net loss is a shift of Tax Burden directly onto the Consumer of the product, and must be subtracted from the price increase of the imported product, due to the placement of tariff. The reduction of Consumer Demand and Consumption of tariffs reduce substantially under this consideration, as otherwise; Consumers would be left with addition of the Tax Burden. Free Trade analogy suffers from refusal to recognize the shift of Tax Burden by foreign production to the domestic Consumer.

The Revisionist Economic argument as to the ineffectiveness of tariffs also ignore the impact of Tax Burden shift. The tariff recoups the loss of taxation by foreign production, and realigns placement of the Tax Burden. The reduction of value of foreign products due to the rise in value of domestic currency brings advantage to the domestic economy, as it also lowers the cost raw materials necessary in domestic production. This re-orders the context of the tariff, turning into a reduction of production costs for domestic performance. The tariff becomes a factor in cheaper domestic production. The Revisionist argument as to the ineffectiveness of tariffs is nullified to the extent of the value of reduced domestic production costs.

The whole complex of Trade remains a very difficult area to assess, in terms of economic benefit. The Author believes intrinsically any level of Trade above the level of Raw Materials contains economic inefficiency, due to the Transportation costs associated with the Trade. The trouble comes in the form that domestic employment and profitability in such Transportation, must be considered as economic growth; whose value must be subtracted from the Transportation Costs of foreign production, above the level of needed foreign raw materials. The Transportation Costs must again be increased by the amount of growth of domestic production occasioned by elimination of unnecessary importation of foreign goods.

The World, Today, probably transfers almost forty percent more Goods as is actually necessary to transport; though One must remember the necessary transfer of raw materials. The Fuel consumption by this excess transfer of Goods, plus the real Capital Equipment and Labor Costs of such transfer, make this a high elemental Cost. The Process, though, provides a huge component to the Transportation Sector; probably providing almost one-third of the profitability of the Transportation sectors involved. This must be counteracted by the misplacement of economic effort by such Capital Equipment and Labor. Total economic inefficiency evaluation of this unnecessary transfer of Goods defies quantification; the Author still estimates this inefficiency costs the World Economy at least one-quarter Trillion dollars a year, an amount with could be translated completely into added Production Profits and Wages to the respective economies.

The Author favors the argument of the Protectionists more than the Free Traders, for the sole rationale; tariffs can be utilized to eliminate unnecessary transfer of Goods. The entire dispute will not be resolved without a serious delineation of the constraints of the Issue, and serious Economic studies to evaluate all economic costs of the current system. The problem remains because of this lack of delineation and study.

❖   ❖   ❖   ❖   ❖

A real feature of tariffs enable use of them for the practice of discrimination of trading partners. All have heard of the term 'Most Favored Nation', which stipulates the Nation is free from the normal range of tariffs. A more evolved form is what is know as the Custom Unions. These comprise a group of nations who agree among themselves to maintain common external tariffs towards all not in the Custom Union, and reduced or no tariffs in trade between themselves. The EEU and NAFTA are basically Custom Unions, though NAFTA does not express the stringency of EEU. Custom Unions are effective at building Trade between the members of the Union, though they illicit higher Consumer prices in the member nations in the short-run; though these costs are reduced in the long-run, through Capital development within the Union.

The World Trade Organization (WTO) seeks to remove the barriers to Trade, though it specifically allows the creation of Custom Unions. The basic lack of viability in the WTO comes from the allowance of these Custom Unions, and the extreme regulation of Agreements made. The major industrial Traders suffer from severe constraints of Trade practice, all produced by the majority rule process of Agreement passage; while ambiguity of Agreement language permits the less prominent trading Nations to ignore the basic rules, when those rules limit their Trade advantage. The major trading Nations feel increasing pressure to abrogate many sections of the aforesaid Agreements, in the face of Third World nations not living up to the Agreements.

The upshot of Custom Unions and the WTO has become they are restrictive in Trade, though remain due to the fact of being advantageous to international Corporations. This advantage derives from Corporate ability to produce in Countries in violation of the Agreements, and sell this Product in Nations observing the Agreements. This allows Corporations to reap economic profits, in excess of normal production products. The practice, itself, is a constraint of Trade, leading to reduction of the total volume of Trade. The speech and ideology of these Organizations remain Free Trade, but the practice becomes increasingly Protectionist; with discrimination towards the major trading nations, who lose jobs with an adverse Cash Flow out of their Countries.

The entire conceptionalism of tariffs intends constraint of Trade. Custom Unions will prove economically unviable, due to Capital development which dictates internal discrimination against Trade. This simply states member nations lose the advantage of this combination rapidly, under the conditions of capitalization allows in the Custom Union. The advantage of trading with a larger Market also grows with the extension of Capitalization. The Author estimates the EEU will not last thirty years in it's present form, as production ratios are expected to grow by four percent per year under the Custom Union. The machinery of the World Trade Organization has lasted longer than the Author estimated, and it's disadvantages continue to grow.

4
Other Transportation Taxes

The most common Transportation tax resides in the Fuel tax, though most Economists would consider it to be an Excise tax; a concept accepted as Utilities begin to charge a Fuel charge to their Customers. There are numerous other Transportation taxes, most notably fare taxes on air travel, railroads, and busses; to acquire some of the passenger income; and the truck Permits and Overweight charges for overloaded vehicles. The Tourist Income is mined through Park Permits and licences. Individual travelers pay through road tolls, licencing fees, fuel taxes, and Wheel taxes. Government generates a multiplex tax system to charge Taxpayers at least a minimum 8–10% of their total Transportation cost as tax.

The Fuel tax contains a major revenue for Government in all industrialized nations. It is solely an economic profit demanded by Government, over and above the normal production cost schedule. It's placement, therefore, acts as a restraint of production; introducing higher production costs unrelated to production itself. The sheer position of the Fuel tax within the production process interjects an overall production loss of what the Author estimates as nine percent of total productivity. The Author estimates the cost to individual Taxpayers because of this positioning, remains a greater loss to them than would be the loss of their personal Income tax exemption under current tax law.

The rationale for Fuel taxes stands as reduction of total usage of limited resource. This proves to be a fallacy, when considering the advance of technology. Improvement in Transport performance has reduced Fuel consumption faster, than has expected restrictions on Fuel usage from taxation. Several Economic studies suggest Consumer travel could not increase more than eight percent of the maximum travel usage of the year 2000. Total miles traveled has been dropping since that time, because of Terrorism, reaction to Terrorism, and the difficulties of travel. There is evidence (still only quite tentative) that the issuance of Drivers' Licences are starting to drop. Economic reports indicate Household personal transport milage is reducing due to the aging of the Population, along with increase of the Workweek for younger member of the Households. Reduction of Fuel tax levels would not likely increase Fuel consumption over present levels.

The Argument to reduce Fuel taxes suggests it would reduce Cargo transport cost by about 1.27 dollars for every dollar reduction of Fuel tax revenue. Actual Fuel consumption depends upon factors other than Fuel cost, and is not expected to increase more than eight percent over the year 2000 usage as said. Actual Productivity increases can be expected to increase by $.87 cents for every dollar reduction in Fuel tax revenue, over the long-run. This does not deny Government would have to raise replacement revenue through other taxation, it simply insists there are more economically-efficient forms of taxation; which do not restrict Productivity.

The Airline industry currently suffers from over-capitalization and constriction of traffic through over-crowded Airports. Terrorist fright has produced Security precautions which simply further constrict Airports, while air traffic is down due to fear. Such considerations are slowly impacting other forms of mass transit, and will continue to grow. Fare taxes serve only as Government subsidy, doing relatively nothing to restrict or expand mass transit usage. Incentives for traffic pattern changes must be of a form other than fuel taxes; the most necessary being the curtailment of number of flights. Air traffic should be reduced by thirty percent for safety, and fifty percent for economic reasons; it being a basically cost-ineffective form of travel.

Bus systems require less than twenty percent of the Capitalization of an airline, for twelve times the route miles covered. Subsidy of Bus fares could multiply bus traffic by four, with only thirty percent of the Security difficulty. Railroads cost as much to capitalize as Air traffic, but require the least fuel of any form of traffic; all within the context of greatest safety and comfort for Passengers. On-board rest accommodations for both forms of transport, could quadruple Passenger traffic for both systems. Labor costs for both forms of transit stand approximately half that of Airlines. This is one area where Government regulation of traffic proves more viable than taxation.

[This is not to state travel volume should not reduce; this reduction best gained by reduction of Traveler income through taxation, as is explained later. The above specifically pressured shifts of traffic patterns between forms of transportation.]

Car and Driver licencing fees are major Transportation taxes, and are areas where taxes should be increased. Increases in either would impel some transfer to mass transit facilities, and go far to elimination of a Fuel tax. Proper implementation could possess added benefits. This Author has long desired mandatory Insurance of all vehicles. This could be accomplished by sufficient high tax on both Cars and Drivers' licences, as to cover the cost of Insurance. Such a Plan would need certain characteristics.

States and Federal Government would have to set limits on Putative Damages allowed in Accident suits, based upon lost years of Individual income. Insurance policies would have to cover all medical corrections expenses, plus limited Putative damage awards. States would sell Personal Liability insurance by competitive bidding to Insurers by License number. Car Liability would be issued by vehicle identification number. Personal Liability would cover all medical costs. Car Liability would cover all Property damage. Unlicenced Drivers would be subject to Prison time, while uninsured vehicles would be confiscated. Vehicles would have an annual tax covering insurance of the vehicle, to get it licensed. Personal drivers would have to provide a Credit Card number, which would be billed monthly. Failure to license or maintain payment would entail State-employed law enforcement officers, whose duty would be to search out all uninsured vehicles, or drivers without license; and compel their observance to the law. These officers would be paid by surcharge to the licensing taxes.

Tourist Park Permits and Licenses for use of facilities should be increased, propelling full payment for upkeep be paid by these taxes. This holds the benefit of limiting usage of the facilities to those who would chose to pay. Maintenance costs of the facilities could be expected to halve the current costs under such a tax; most Users can afford the use of the Parks, but would discontinue multiple yearly use. Overall Government tax burden would be reduced, and the ecology of the Parks preserved. The Change would probably be lauded by most Users, though there will initial objection.

Uniform weight and length standards for Cargo transport should be implemented on the national level. Tonnage and length could be lessened for reasons of safety, and less wear on the Community-supplied access. Increases in Transport cost and lowered Wages in the industry, would be counteracted by increases in the Transport labor force, and greater Profits in the Transport-Support industries. Fuel increases would be minimal, as Shippers adopted the most Cost-effective venue of transport. Wages in the Transport industry could be expected to slide no more than twelve percent, while Labor hours would be expected to increase by sixteen percent. Capital maintenance costs for road and railway can be expected to decrease by twenty percent. Consumer product price increases can be expected not to exceed an overall increase of two percent. Proper usage of transport would not increase road and railway construction. The loss of Government revenues from overweight charges can be replaced by other taxation.

5
Licensing Fees and Service Charges.

Government charges for Permits, Licenses, and use of Government services made up much of the revenue of Government, in the first half of this Country's history. Entrance into the Twentieth Century brought limitation to this practice, mainly through the demands of the Progressive Movement for equality of Government access for Citizens. Such Charges were reduced to at most a recovery of supply expenses. The tone of the Country altered with the inauguration of Ronald Reagan, who wished to reduce obvious, direct taxes; States followed suit with an increase of such fees.

This trend continues to advance at the present time, with some Counties already charging an Assessor fee to assess homes; after which residential property tax will be assessed. Building Permits and Inspections have been going up in price, with the numbers of such mandatory Permits and Inspections on the increase. Official Copies of documentation has been increasing in Price, over and above actual costs. Vehicle licensing has actually gone down in cost, but pricing, without addition of service, has exceeded the Inflation rate. The same can be said for various Recreational licenses—Hunting, Fishing, Boating, etc. A noted area of reduction is in the writing of Speeding tickets to Motorists, since the Insurance companies use of these Tickets to raise already high insurance rates; bringing huge Driver denunciation of the practice.

The activity of the Judicial branch of Government at all three levels, has been the forerunner on charging User taxes. Court practice becomes increasingly expensive, to the point where an Applicant needs a lawyer to simply front the money to start a Suit. Every Court filing carried a Charge, and One designed solely to support the budget of the Court. Some Individual lawyers have been known to pay two thousand dollars per month in such charges. Large Law Firms can pay up to a quarter-million dollars per month. This may seem incredible to Anyone used to their little County Courthouse, but it probably ingests two million dollars per year, in Fines, Court Costs, Filing Charges, and License fees per year.

Liquor and Tobacco licenses make up a huge net revenue for States across the Country. A friend of the Author related how his license fees for a Bar and Tobacco shop exceeded his monthly rent; said location with the highest property taxes in the City. These are specifically not the Excise taxes imposed on these Items. He also complained about the Employer Withholding Tax to provide for Worker Unemployment benefits; claiming the State directed thirty percent of such funds to the general revenue, which it did. This was all on top of a City Business license, whose price varied by location; and City Access fees charged for City-owned parking garages. The Individual's story was little different than those of other Retailers in the Country.

The total Tax component of such after-expense Tax component fees probably make up 14–16% of City revenues, and about eight percent of State revenues. They are on the increase, both in total price and in share of fee which is Tax. They also make up at least twenty percent of the regulatory paperwork, which businesses must fill out. The two elements of paperwork plus fees probably make up about eleven percent of the operating costs of American retail business.

The Construction industry faces unknown numbers of fees with contain a Tax component, making up a significant operating expense: there are Plan submission fees, Utility search fees, Utility access fees, Copy fees for building plans, building permit fees, building permit stamps, Inspection fees, and construction permit fees. Almost all have at least a twenty percent Tax component associated with such fees. The list does not end with the above features; almost all construction today requires Environment Impact studies and Construction Cleanup Inspections. The submission of an Environmental Impact study have submission fees, with later Acceptance Stamp fees. Cleanup Inspections almost always carry an arbitrary fine for lack of perfection; this added to the price of the Inspection itself. This process is not only expensive, with major component of Tax; but brings delays in construction schedules of high prices in terms of labor charges, capital equipment cost delays, etc.

Study of History indicates Licensing and Service Charge fees increase with the bureaucracy of the Government, and the Tax component of such fees tend to increase. The greatest rationale for this is the indirectness of the Tax; a simple economic expression of the fact, most of the impact of the taxes can be hidden from the general public. Those who directly pay the tax cannot complain, because of direct impact on their Incomes by interruption of licensing approval; while such tax can be passed onto the public, by increases in Product pricing. The impact of these fees can be expected to worsen.

6

Property Tax

The concept of Property tax would seem to be most fair, charging those who have possession of the Property. The fairness of the Property tax has been challenged throughout the history of the Tax; with arguments which have significant actuality. Simple assessment does not effectively evaluate the actual value of the Property, fails to equalize the tax on the basis of capital development, and ignores the actual return Rental value of this capitalization. People with less capital return on the Property, must pay an equivalent tax with those who make higher returns. The tax is thereby regressive in nature, with those making less paying a greater percentage share of the tax.

Current use of the Property tax creates greater inequity. Business with greater political clout than ordinary citizenry, get immunities from the Property tax; through the advent of Fee-Trade zones and relocation allowances. Residential property-holders and small business pay for these tax breaks, through higher assessment rates on their own properties. These taxpayers suffer from a tax which is not only regressive, but discriminatory.

Traditional Economists believed Property taxes were basically destructive of economic performance. Property assessments did not adequately alter to reflect the varying rates of Rental return on different properties. They also charged larger assessments against Property-holders who thought to improve their property through capitalization. These Economists estimated the property assessment rates pressured for equalization of Rental return rates; thereby, inciting inflationary pressure on both under-developed and developed properties; by differentiation of property quality.

Modern Economists suggest the Property tax actually pressures for capital investment in less-developed properties, so there will be an equalization of Rental return on all property. They are still honest enough to admit there are inherent geographical features which limit the development of property, so there will always be differences in Rental returns. They also admit the factor of location limits the degree of capital development. The animosity to Property taxes has subsided, though, because of the near universal use of Property taxes by Governments. They perceive Property tax as essential for payment of basic Government services, which would require alternate taxes to pay for, if dismissed.

Analysis of the Property tax, itself, expresses an archaic nature to the tax. The tax presupposes an Rental return for property, which is hard to visualize in the area of Residential property. The Household installed on the site is mystically inspired to provide some Rental return to the property as Household expense, even when the Household holds title to the property. A tax assessment thereby is legitimate. The Author wonders how a Household payment to itself can derive another expense to itself. Economics often reminds of Astrology.

The reality stands most property consigned to pay property tax does not derive a Rental return income. The property should not be taxed. Many now will think the discussion becomes only a game of Semantics, but the argument holds many Economic model characteristics; which will vastly alter the collection of taxes, and the total value of such taxes. The resultant will affect the nature of Economic growth.

A Title-Holding tax should replace the Property tax. This Tax should be a percentage of the original purchase price of the Property, plus all capital improvements put into the property, plus any yearly inflationary rate which has been generated through the years since purchase. Why the necessity for change, when it seems to equate to a

Property tax? It really does not! A property tax alludes to a mythical existence of some intrinsic value, the Title-Holding tax evaluates a real value for the Property, with positioning to introduce depreciation losses to existent value. Almost all property will revert to a lower evaluation and assessment based upon actual values of the property. The economic rationale states Property tax only evaluates the value of the Property, while a Title-Holding tax evaluates the process of capitalization of the Property; assessing the gain and loss of value.

Depreciation of Property value will lead to lowered taxation, potential source of saved capitalization of the Property. Increased capitalization will induce higher tax, which will limit capitalization to where it is advantageous economically; while Maintenance costs will be reduced through deprecation evaluations. The Reader will likely dismiss this economic analysis as unimportant; but deprecation allowances would ease Capitalization expenses by about four percent, lengthen periods between remodeling by an average twenty months, and cut Maintenance costs by an average twenty percent. The shift is not unimportant to Taxpayers, while the average quality of the Property will not change.

The above alteration will have little impact unless the method of payment for Government services is arranged differently. The Author will discuss elsewhere a proposition to separate provision for Education facilities from any form of Property tax. The Government provision of roadway, utilities, and sewage must be transferred to a Services mortgage payable monthly, based on a thirty-year mortgage of the expense. The mortgage will be real, as the Government finances through Private lending institutions; with the Title-holders of the specified Property being the named Mortgage-holder. The mortgages will be accretionary, in that future maintenance charges will be added to the mortgage. The Title-holding tax will be limited to payment of law enforcement, municipal government expenses, and street-cleaning (Snow removal, etc.) expenses. The Property-holder will only be responsible for his direct use of Government services, in a program which will reduce the Community debt.

Most Homeowners would say such alteration would not make an appreciable difference to their payments. Nothing could be further from the truth. Commercial demands on Utilities which are in excess of Residential needs, and must be borne by the Commercial enterprise itself; in a mortgage which it must pay. This is the same with road networks of greater durability for commercial traffic. Proven depreciation of property will gain reduction of the assessment tax. Personal improvements will bring increase. Capital expenditures of your neighbors will not entail capital expenditures on your own part. The Property-holder becomes solely liable only for his own property.

Tax revenues will increase; while collection costs and Community burden will decrease. Seventy percent of local government debt load can be Privatized, with improvement of Community services; and Property-holders find greater ease of payment, with only normal Interest charges common to the Private Sector. The inequality of the Property tax will be eliminated, with Commercial properties paying the same usage rates as Residential properties; based upon actual usage costs of the specific property. Local Government out-sources it's debt load, without the commitment Interest charges; lowering the eventual Tax rates.

Economic evaluations of the alteration can only be rational guesses, in the absence of statistical studies. Divorce of the Educational burden from local property tax base would reduce existent Property taxes by an average thirty percent. Out-sourcing of finance for roadway and sewage would reduce the existent Property tax by about eleven percent. The switch to a Title-Holders' tax should cut the current Property tax by 7–12% additionally. The Privatization of Services mortgages should increase the Property-holders' liability by about 28% of the current value of their Property payable by a thirty-year mortgage; which also reduces their listed assets and resell value of their property. The Community would still be responsible for whatever Debt load could not be collected by private financial institutions; who hold the mortgages.

The average Property-holder could potentially find his local tax rates cut by almost one-half; with a probable increase in his monthly mortgage payment of about 15–30%. The mortgage payments could still be deductible under current Income tax law as acceptable expense reduction of Income. Yearly depreciation rates may cancel any inflationary rates, and possibly provide real-value reduction in local tax. The Community government gains from removal of Debt load, and escape from Interest payments thereby.

The above analysis may seem to waffle, this due to the fact: the method of specific implementation can alter a gain for Property-holders into a minus; this by the specific nature of the legislation. Enactment which does not equalize Expense Burden between Residential and Commercial properties will increase the Burden for Residential properties. Alteration, even without Commercial properties paying their fair share, could still provide benefit to Residential Property-holders; this coming from ease of payment considerations, and the compilation of debt into Household debt. The added interest of the mortgage can be canceled by restrictions of property tax increases.

7

Excise Taxes

Traditional Economists placed great faith in Excise taxes, believing them far superior to direct taxes; such as Property, Head, or Income taxes. They are nothing more than a per item tax placed on the manufacturer or the distributor of Products. Much literature exists considering the many issues associated with Excise Taxes. A great deal concerns the debate on whether such Taxes should be broad-based on many or most items, or concentrated on a few necessity items to produce the most revenue. There was general agreement on the need of Excise taxes and Customs taxes to conform; Customs being an older term for tariffs. Current Economic thought on Excise taxes has adopted the formula of 'Sin tax' on a few high-revenue generation items.

Excise taxes contain many attractive elements, plus several disadvantages. The risk is always present such taxes will be used to penalize immorality, as is established with the American liquor and tobacco excise taxes. High excise tax rate gets passage, with repeal extremely hard; because of the sheer revenues gained for the Government. Such tax turns highly regressive upon those whose lifestyle becomes impacted. Attempts to equalize the Tax Burden remain futile, in the face of legislative desire to spend. The Author has thought to equalize impact of Excise taxation, by spreading the base of items; believing Coffee, Tea, and Soft Drinks should be included in the base taxed by Excise.

More detailed Economic study finds Excise taxes constrict Consumer Demand, but at a rate far less than the dollar value of revenues gained; possibly less than Sales taxes, which are charge directly on the Consumer at time of purchase. They also tend to restrict Product pricing to induce economic profits, because they accelerate Consumer Demand reduction. The tax is regressive, as universally more of poorer Income purchase in total volume; than do the purchase volumes of higher Income. The regression, though, is somewhat proportional as higher Incomes tend to purchase more of individual product through ability to pay. The Excise tax, if properly imposed, could actually be more progressive than the current Income Tax.

Real advantage in the American case could be gained by implementation of an Entertainment Tax, which would include the liquor and tobacco Excise taxes; but also tax movie and theater tickets, concert tickets, gambling and Lottery tickets, and Sporting events tickets. All are high income generative industries with high inelasticity of price, so substantial revenues could be gained. The current prices of such items today, assure the excise taxes would be paid by those who can pay the tickets; this turns such taxes progressive. A sufficiently high Excise on gambling and Lottery tickets should reduce the regressiveness of such revenue collections at present.

Tentative Economic studies, with lack of solid conclusiveness, suggest Excise taxes reduce Middleman profit-taking at a faster progression than the level of revenue; this means that for every dollar of Excise tax, there is a somewhat greater than a dollar reduction of Middleman profits. This could provide restraint to Middleman Costs, which have been increasing faster than Production Costs and Retail Costs. This contains concern as Middleman Costs express the highest Profits per volume of the three Cost schedules, with the lowest Overhead Costs; as well as the highest Profit per Labor hour ratio. Curtailment of Middlemen Profits remains a must, if Inflationary pressure is to be removed.

The Author speculates the possibility a judicious program of Excise taxes could actually result in lower Product prices, if certain conditions were met. The Excise tax base would have to be set on items of greater utilization to higher Income, than to lower Income. Food items for the Excise tax base could be taken from the major entre dishes of an upper-class restaurant. Liquor excise could be limited to only those which occupy the upper half of a Price Bell Curve. The same could be done with tobacco products. An alternative could be a progressive excise tax—set at a percentage of Retail list price of the item, listed as so much per dollar. Above-normal fee schedules could be established for Entertainment tickets.

The most pressing need for an Excise tax in this Country resides in taxation of charitable contributions. All Tax-paying entities in this Country utilize such contributions to reduce their taxable income. Fund-raising costs of Charitable organizations have been raising constantly, with reducing remittance to the proclaimed Cause of collection. Most major Charity officers make more than their Congressmen, Senators, Governors, or Presidents. The remuneration of fund-raising are proportionably as generous. They achieve this because of the tax deduction effect of contributions. An Excise tax of twelve percent of all Charity contributions must be passed, to forestall the loss of Tax revenues from other tax systems. The law should also stipulate half of all contributions must go to the professed Cause of the Charity, else tax deduction status is lost.

The Author has several other specialized uses for Excise taxes, which will be discussed in later Chapters. The Economic student should realize Excise taxes are like all other tax systems, with advantages and disadvantages. Any program of taxation need utilize the full venue of tax kind, in order to implement a fair program. One must institute every kind of tax to maximize it's benefits, and minimize it's liabilities. Taxes are only a reflection of the variety of the Economy, with it's multiplex of payment conditions.

Excise taxes, like tariffs, have gained a bad reputation amongst current Economic theorists. Most of the derision is undeserved. The greatest advantage of both of the above lies in ability to regulate uniformity of Price between Products in the Economy. Steak can become excessively expensive in relationship to a replacement product—Hamburger. The rationale for this excess being the prices of cattle, which cause packing plants to fully utilize Product; expecting to make their Profit off the sale of expensive meats.

The prices for cattle result from the limitation of the numbers of cattle, due to high charges of operating capital for Feeders, and the high cost of processed Feed for the cattle. A high Excise tax on Steak would cause Meat-packers to purchase even less beef. The price of Hamburger would rise, as a reduction of beef purchase lowers Hamburger supply faster than Steak supply; and the demand for Steak has switched to Hamburger. Feeders would find lower cost finance service and oversupply of beef, and processed Feed manufacturers would have surplus production. The higher price of Hamburger would incite Packers to purchase more cattle which would be lower in price, Feeders would expand their capacity back to normal, processed Feed would remain lower in price because of the greater elasticity in cattle price structure; while Feeders would be paying higher prices to Ranchers and Farmers to gain more cattle, causing them to raise more head of cattle.

The effect of the Excise tax on Steak brought a lower price for Steak, a higher price for Hamburger, more cattle slaughtered by Packers, more cattle raised by Rancher and Feeders, and more processed feed for the cattle at cheaper price. Interest rates on operating capital for the entirety of the beef industry went down, after initial normal delays. Consumers pay a higher price for Hamburger, but get a greater supply of it; with ability to defray cost to their Consumption budget with the purchase of replacement product Steak, at lowered prices.

Consideration of the regressiveness of the Excise tax on Steak finds the burden of the Tax borne by the higher Income classes, while the increases in Hamburger price will fall with the greater supply of beef products. Many would suggest the economic impact will be only temporary, but evidence proves this to be untrue. Hamburger price will not totally reduce, and Steak will maintain resistence to the Excise tax being passed on to the Consumer. Meat-packers, Feeders, Processed Feed manufacturers, and Ranchers will want to maintain the higher production levels, because of the marginal Profit per Unit. The Excise tax on Steak will maintain a higher beef production over time.

This effect of Excise taxes can be noted in many industries. Excise taxes on the luxury items produced by the industry, will maintain heightened production of replacement products in the industry. An Excise tax on Cadillacs will produce increased production of Chevy; this done with price rise less on Cadillacs than the Excise tax, without appreciable rise in the price of a Chevy. Excise taxes on luxury items can thereby incite replacement product production increases, with only marginal Price increases. The production of luxury items is reduced, and lower Incomes actually rise in relation to higher Income brackets.

Excise taxes can also produce uniformity of Price between Products of no relation (neither Complementary or Replacement products). Excise taxes on Entertainment items can not only increase the Work-weeks of Labor, but increase Consumer Demand for unrelated Products. There is the famous Economic Case of the increase in Professional Baseball ticket prices increasing the number of Sales of Lawnmowers. Increases in Restaurant prices will increase the sale of Video movies. Increased Theme Park ticket prices will raise membership in Softball teams, with increased attendance of their games. Increased membership pricing in Physical Fitness Centers will increase Sales of walking shoes, Outdoor clothing, and use of Parks.

This type of Tax best controls monopoly pricing better than any other tax. The placement of a stiff Excise on monopoly-produced items will decrease Demand for such Product, sharply reducing marginal per item profit. This reduced Profit removes monopoly ability to stop entry into the production sector, while encouraging efficient production along normal production cost scheduling due to the high Retail price. Most Economists would disagree on this Issue, but it reduced Capitalization cost in relation to Retail Item price; with the Tax considered as a normal production cost.

Excise tax can be used by Government economic programs to fuel industrial sectors which are showing slower growth than others, through excise tax placement on products of overheated Sectors. This reduces production in the overheated Sector, transfers Consumer Demand to other Sectors, and fuels capitalization of under-achieving Sectors. The value of use of Excise rather than Government supports of deflated Sectors comes in the lessened expenditure of Government funds, actually increase of Government revenue, plus actual increase in Consumer Demand; this coming from increased employment in Sectors without excise taxation. The increased Product prices of the Sectors with excise do not antagonize financial operating instruments in the taxed Sector; as the excise tax does not affect the actual marginal profitability of Unit product. Excise tax can be the least intrusive of Government economic regulation, if properly handled.

The original argument against Excise taxes was the difficulty of collection of the revenues. This defect has been removed with the computerization of the modern economy. The near universal Sales Tax suffers from much greater defects of collection. The purported hidden nature of the excise tax also must be discounted, due to the modern Consumer's inability to track even his ordinary Household expenses. The Author has a mother who forgot she had one Insurance policy, which had been automated pay from a financial account. No mortgage holder can immediately state what he pays monthly for Insurance on the loan. The Author, himself, cannot visualize the itemized bill of his electric company. He doubts communication with the Utility would help with his understanding. He also doubts the hidden nature of an Excise charge would matter in a very complicated World.

Almost every charge upon the individual Household today remains indirect. The advent of IRAs with their tax delays ensure no one can establish their exact worth, it once taking a Probate court thirty-seven years to bring down judgement of the exact worth of a deceased individual. The IRS is still trying to determine the assets of John Gotti, long a resident of a Federal prison, and recently deceased. A Construction Executive once filed Suit against a Government agency, sole purpose being to get a Statement from the Agency on how much they claimed to have paid him towards a construction project; three months later, Judge and Agency said they would accept any reasonable claim he made on the Agency. The confusion goes on; Excise taxes could not increase the confusion.

Excise is a tax system too easily dismissed. Collection has a general history of capability, without the variation of Income, Property, or even Sales taxes. The Revenues are consistent, though constrained by growth in the Economy, which translates as Consumer Demand must be constant or increasing. Revenues from Excise drop under Recessive conditions. Excise tax can present specific economic regulation, unlike almost any other form of Government activity. The regressive nature of Excise taxes can be modified through the method of item selection. The exercise of the Excise depresses Consumer Demand less than almost any other form of taxation, considering the level of tax; basically, it only amends the Consumers' choice, without significantly reducing his purchase decision. The Author likes the Excise tax.

[The important point for the Student to remember is that Governmental revenues have to be obtained, if Government spending programs are to be maintained. The choice is not whether to tax, as the Funds must flow. The real question is how the taxes are to be collected. The method of collection can be far worse on the Economy, than is the simple extraction of revenues. Placement of Tax Burden can ruin the economic viability of specific Income classes, both poor and wealthy; through the difficulty created for the class functioning in the economic sense. A bombardment sequence to taxation can be created, where Taxpayers are periodically deprived of necessary operating funds. Tax programs can unintentionally transfer Tax impact, so Taxpayers escape or are overtaxed. The Economist must first determine what a tax system is doing, before he can alter economically disadvantageous effects.]

8

The Added-Value Tax

A much discussed form variation of an Excise tax is the added-value tax. This has all the spread of a broad-based Excise tax where a wide range of products are taxed. It differs from the Excise tax in that it is placed on various stages of a Product's development, with taxation at each stage of development. It taxes each stage only on the increase of value brought to the product from that particular stage. This tax is almost always a percentage tax, but one which subtracts the start-value of the Product or materials, prior to estimate of the tax. Many Economists find this method of taxation fascinating, as it is a truly indirect tax; where Consumers cannot determine where product cost leaves off, and tax starts.

The process starts with Government transforming the image of itself, conceptionalizing itself as a form of super-business. Government, under this Concept, has the right and ability to draw profit from all Operations inside it's jurisdiction. The added-value tax becomes in-line profits-taking, as Government has the purported right to profit from all operations inside it's territory. The added-value tax finds increasing use in Europe, but faces American opposition.

Purely Economic thought would state Government had nothing to do with the capitalization of the operations, which the Government would tax. Government, therefore, has no right to the profits-sharing of the enterprises involved. The Government gains right to share in the success of the enterprise involved with the added-value tax, but escapes from the financial service of the capitalization; not even to mention evasion of any loss from operation. The added-value tax becomes an added cost to business operation, without the Government supplying debt service, or bearing any part of the risk-taking. The added-value tax weakens business resiliency, while raising operating costs at every stage of Production.

The Author has great animosity towards in-line profits-taking, known to Anyone who has read his tract: INFLATION: ROOTS OF EVIL. In-line profits-taking magnifies all operating costs, from raw materials to final Retail Sale. It is the leading inflationary pressure, even exceeding resource scarcity as source of Inflation. The added-value tax has a universality which crosses the entirety of the Economy. This totality forestalls all traditional outlets to release inflationary pressure before Price Increase. Discount Sales of Product canceling normal in-line profits-taking will not have the effect, as before the added-value tax, because this tax revenue cannot be discounted. Production operations which already operate on marginal-profit bases, will come under increasing pressure, where they cannot finance their debt service. High-Profit production operations, whose high profits come from economic-necessity advantage; will be induced to raise in-line production pricing, in order to maintain their Profits schedules.

Analysis of the above information tells Us traditional economic adjustments are stopped by the universality of the added-value tax. These readjustments operate almost continually, realigning Product prices into balance; to forestall Wage inequities from destroyed Labor provision viability. Discount Sales are the median by which worse-positioned Labor maintains Consumer Demand levels equivalent to higher-paid Labor. The added-value tax erodes the value of the discounts; creating pressure for Wage increases in the worse-positioned Labor. Higher-paid Labor insists on maintenance of Wage differentials, so there begins a continuing Wage spiral upward; with the introduction of the added-value tax.

The initial impact of the Wage spiral would be the loss of the discounts by the added-value tax, but the Inflation would quickly brings additional production costs to each operational sector; this raising the value of the product increase per operation, so lifting the revenue of the tax. The increased revenue of the added-value tax would further shrink the discounts offered to worse-positioned Labor elements. It would also raise the real-value cost of Government services by the rate of Inflation, eliminating pressure to reduce the percentage rate of added-value tax.

The economic curve of Product Prices shows not only a total line increase by the percentage revenues of the added-value tax, but a total line increase by the rate of inflation generated by the added-value tax. The only restraint on the rate of Inflation consists on the inelasticity of Wage, not in the worse-positioned Labor quadrant; but in the high-paid Labor quadrant. The economic-necessity advantage of their quadrant is always refueled, as overall Prices increase; reflecting the gain in Wage by the worse-positioned Labor quadrant. This means there is only a delay occasioned with the rate of Inflation, the time differential being only the amount of time necessary to reconstruct the economic-necessity advantage of the high-paid Labor quadrant. Inflation is inescapable under a added-value tax.

Added-value taxation finds favor with Politicians and Economists, because Consumers cannot define or differentiate between Product Cost and Tax. The economic impact of the tax, though, will always pressure for a rate of Inflation which is disadvantageous. The Author lacks the research materials to accurately determine what rates of Inflation would be incurred. An accurate presentation require statistical estimates of the loss of discounts levels, due to the added-value tax increases of product prices.

Casual estimates of the discounts reductions will be presented, and probably derided by statistical Economists. An added-value tax of three percent place upon an Economy with an average of Eight operational steps in Production, leads to a real-value increase in product pricing of

24%. Normal discount rates of Discount Sales make 34% discount of value seem reasonable. The added-value tax reduces the product price for worse-positioned Labor by only ten percent, instead of the normal 34%. This states worse-positioned Labor cannot afford some portion of the discount product price between 1–24% of the price. The decline of their actual purchases may range up to 56%; a determinant of previous studies on rapid failure of income, due to loss of employment.

The intermix of Consumer Goods remains such that forty percent of purchased Goods are effective necessities for worse-positioned Labor; on which they pay a twenty percent overpricing. This translates in to a loss of total value purchase of Goods of Eight percent, because of the added-value tax. Purchase of the remaining Goods will incur a further loss of ten percent of the Goods which they could previously purchase, before the added-value tax. This can functionally translate as a fifteen percent loss in standard of living for the worse-positioned Labor quadrant. This quadrant will immediately pressure for Wage increases which will finance the lost standard of living. The consequence will be an Inflation rate somewhere below five percent per year, but not less than two percent; this taking into account various factors: Management resistence to Wage increases, level of Labor insistence, and the economic norm of three years' gestation to normally exercise economic pressures throughout an economy.

The above analysis is a simple economic model, expressing the pressure from only an individual year of added-value tax impact. This tax actually operates continually, providing acceleration for the already existent rate of Inflation. A Layman can understand the impact of the added-value tax as being a 5–7% Inflation rate after three years' operation of the added-value tax. This can be offset by suppression of Labor Wage demands, but only at a predictable rate of loss of standard of living for Labor; this loss should continue until there is a reduction of about one-quarter of the standard of living for the working classes.

The Author has often been accused of artificially exciting normal economic forces, in order to prove his theses. He has always contended other Economists did not give these forces proper weight, due to their position in the status quo. There is no doubt the added-value tax is a very poor method of taxation, resulting in the destruction of the standard of living of Labor involved in the production process. The orientation of the Economy must be directed toward the expansion of the standard of living for all; otherwise, all will suffer because of loss of Labor capability.

[Lay people could become excessively worried by this discussion. There exists social and political avenues by which adverse economic impacts can be blocked. These are traditionally used whenever losses to the standard of living become too great. This does not obviate the bad economic pressures generated by the added-value tax. Correct positioning of tax systems remain the best regulation of the economy by Governments.]

9

The Sales Tax

Sales tax evolved into the most universal of all types of taxes, practically every Government uses this tax in one form or another. It's appeal lies in the fact it applies to all, with relatively no way to evade it. It possesses support from the upper classes, due to the fact it is a heavy generator of revenue, and draws tax from classes otherwise impossible to tax. This certifies it's place as probably the most regressive tax of them all. It even drafts Welfare recipients, who must purchase on the open market.

This tax relies on a percentage of Consumer purchases, making it a economic suppressant of Consumer Demand; draining off a percentage of disposable income. The reduction of Consumption becomes increasingly important, as percentage rates increase; a factor more vital in many American urban areas, where rates rise to match greater demand for social services. The aging of the Population pertains here, as it is aging fastest in regions with dropping commercial activities and production. Local government seek to avoid debt by expanded Sales tax revenues, rate expansion seriously impacting Retail Sales.

Serious impediment derives from this decision. Higher Sales tax rates only pressure demands to raise welfare allotments, while increasing the maintenance costs of support industries, and the supportive tax base. Actual economic studies of the issue of Sales tax impact are basically unreliable, commissioned by government to justify increased rates. A few ad-hoc studies have considered the issue; one in particular estimating real-value increase in cost to the Tax base with dropping revenue, after rates increase beyond 4.7%. Causation would be marginal increases in welfare payments necessary, with impact reduction of Consumption rates.

The real danger of Sales tax comes from the nature of it's creation. It ordinarily origins in a Sales tax proposal put to the Voters of the government unit, with a realistic percentage rate and dedicated to a universally-supported purpose. The wording of the Enactment, though, places regulation in the hands of some Government organ or body; empowered by the Act, to alter the rate. The Political legislative body expands the purpose, continually widening the government services to be funded by the Sales tax; while the Government supervisory body increases the rate of Sales tax, to provide the revenues demanded. They most generally simply continue raising the rate, when the revenues start to decrease due to falling Consumption.

The regressive nature of the Sales tax also provides real detriment to the lower Income classes. The smaller level of income, combined with necessary provision of basic needs; produces a reaction where Disposable Income of lower incomes declines at almost twice the rate of higher incomes. This means the Consumption of lower incomes drop almost twice as fast under rising Sales tax rates, as do higher incomes. The process is so profound that lower incomes have Consumption rates falling faster than the Sales tax increase, while higher incomes fall slower than the rate increase. This translates into lower incomes lose accelerating fractional percentage above One percent of Consumption, for every percent increase in Sales tax; higher incomes lose a decelerating percentage fractional-point loss for every percent increase in Sales tax.

Another view of this effect could be consideration of the actual working of the tax. A five percent Sales tax will cost $5 per $100 of Goods purchased. The total cost of the Sales tax for Ten Thousand dollars worth of Goods equals $500. Incomes not exceeding $10,000 will reduce Consumption by an actual $700–800 per year. Incomes of

$30,000 per year will actually reduce Consumption by around $300, even though the tax bill is $1500. Incomes above $60,000 may actually increase Consumption, as other forms of taxation are reduced by Sales tax revenue. This reflects the real tax rates to each Income group: leaving real income at $9500, $28,500, and $57,000. Necessity provision remains the same for all three incomes, around $9000. Resultant disposable income stands at $500, $19,500, and $48,000. Impact of the Sales tax costs half of the disposable income of the lowest income, decreases the disposable income of the middle income by 7.6 percent, and decreases the disposable upper income by 6.25 percent.

The total regressive impact of a Sales tax can be seen by the above example. An Economic study once estimated the disposable income had to reach at least thirty percent of total income, before an increase in the standard of living could be realized ($11,700 if necessities stand at $9000 without tax). It made this estimate based upon simple increment in the Basket Goods component, thereby making the findings highly suspect. The Author insists an Income group must achieve an eight percent Savings rate per year, before supported standard of living increases can be realized. The Sales tax leaves the lowest income some $300 short of the necessary Savings rate, with no disposable income at all.

A more illustrative example could be consideration of Consumer loan rates and the Sales tax. An income of $10,000 with a Sales tax of five percent could effectively borrow not more than $3300, which could potentially be doubled with removal of the Sales tax. The income of $30,000 can borrow a potential $130,000 with the Sales tax, only $133,000 with removal of the Sales tax. It is obvious the Sales tax cuts the disposable income of the Poor, actively cutting their ability to borrow to capitalize, and cancels their potential for economic advancement. This is most drastically true in the funding of Education and training for job improvement. The Sales tax serves as an impediment to the provision of future labor reserves.

The Reader probably thinks the Sales tax is an evil Demon by this time, which is not exactly true. It continues because it effectively funds a wide range of government services, with ease of tax collection and largesse of revenues. It allows for suppression of Property tax assessment increases, and thereby; stops inflation of Consumer product prices pushed by Commercial property Overhead Costs. This can effectively be estimated to halve the actual Sales tax rate applied almost anywhere. Studies have indicated Welfare recipients will flow to areas of low Sales tax rates, if welfare payments will follow. Sales taxes thereby become a safety net for local governments, reducing their welfare payments cost. They have saving graces!

The regressiveness of the Sales tax, though, forestalls improvement of the economic condition of lower incomes; while allowing higher incomes to pay less tax than they would otherwise pay. The regressive nature of the Sales tax deeply restricts the ability of lower incomes to capital improvements of their standard of living. The distribution spread between highest and lowest income classes continues to grow; the Sales tax a heavy factor in that growth. The Sales tax serves as a system for higher income classes to evade taxation, effectively overtaxing lower income classes. Higher income classes could expect to pay around 210 percent of their current Sales tax payment, if assessment was in a more progressive tax form.

This over taxation of lower income classes has serious economic defects. Loss of revenue precludes all incomes below about $25,000 per year, from gaining approximately $3000 of Consumer credit; realistically, probably limited to about $2000 of actual Consumer Demand increase. Total increase of Consumer Demand could be found by multiplying $2000 times the number of Households making $25,000 or below. This level of Consumption would require a vast reduction of the Unemployment rolls, and make Business imagine they were in the mid-1990s once more. There is a real rationale for rolling back Sales tax rates, with substitution of other revenue-bearing taxes; which have less impact upon Consumption rates.

[Notice the above argument did not rely on traditional Economic analysis, which simply equates a dollar for dollar reduction of Consumption; due to the Sales tax. Students of Economics need understand the in-line flow of economic forces. The magnitude changes on Consumer Demand from Sales taxes are much greater than a simple reduction of Consumer buying dollars. The real effect resides in what they do, or don't do; because of this loss in disposable income.

Consumption may be viewed as reduced by close to a trillion dollars, because of the lack of Consumer credit extension caused by the Sales tax. Business makes decisions based on the reduced level of Consumption; content with the loss of billions of dollars of Profits. A probable 50–70 billion dollars of Wages are not earned, at levels which are much above the lowest income levels. This induces added loss of Consumer credit extension, and accelerating loss of Consumption.

The Author perceives an increase of seven percent in welfare payments cost, for every percentage increase in Sales tax rate average Nationwide. He could not present effective evidence to substantiate his belief, lacking accurate statistical research materials and Staff. There is much evidence, though, that welfare payments expand faster under Sales tax rate increases above 4.7%, than the increase of revenues by these increases. He calls upon the Economic research organizations to investigate this area, and publish their results.]

10
Welfare-Insurance Taxes

Much study has been done of late years into the replacement of Personal Income taxes with Social Security taxes for lower income classes. The essential thesis states the level of these assessments easily replace previously impacting Income taxes. The Economists involved claim it is effectively forcing the lower income classes to fund their own welfare payment system, without adequate compensation from those benefitting from the economic performance. The Author will herein state forcing people to provide for themselves is not economically unsound, but enjoinment of lower income classes to pay for unusual social expenses is unsound. This is what is being done, and need be examined.

The problem revolves around the fact all funds are placed in a general fund, but divided dispersal levels are drawn from this fund. There are limitation levels of tax beyond which Taxpayers do not pay, yet; there are differentiation levels of dispersal based upon how much has been paid. Equality could be maintained, if the limitation levels of tax payment conformed to the levels of dispersal. They most certainly do not! Definition of the problem would be the limitation levels are determined by purported dispersal levels, but do not account for the provision of medical services; which Congress entitled to be withdrawn from the general fund.

Medicare and Medicaid payments continue to increase as total percentage of dispersals, in an economic environment where the medical industry have the fastest-growing Costs in the Economy. Accelerating medical costs in the above programs nullify the differentials of payment levels, as no one under the current payment schedule funds their own medical insurance in the program. The lowest income classes, with the least elasticity of disposable income, receive discrimination in dispersal payments; though all classes fail to fund their total insurance. The lower income classes only utilize about 79% of the total medical payments per individual, as do the upper-income levels. This means the lower income classes actually pay more of their income for insurance under the program, and receive less payment and insurance from it; both in terms of received benefits, and inability to fund co-payments.

Co-payments for medical procedures stand as the current legislative attempt of lower the medical expense to the Social Security general fund. The regressive nature of this tax, and it is a tax; comes in the restriction of medical services to those who cannot pay. It reduces the provision of medical services to half of Social Security recipients, simply because the recipients cannot match the co-payments demanded. It stands as excise tax to prevent medical use, simply demanding such tax be paid directly to the medical service provider. It effectively negates provision of medical services of major cost to those who cannot pay for supplementary insurance. The cost of supplementary insurance premiums continue to rise, further excluding use; reaching levels much in excess of normal Social Security taxation for Workers as Payroll deductions.

The increasing cost of the medical side of Social Security demands alteration of both collection of revenue, and provision of benefits. The first aspects finds resistence from Taxpayers generally, Economists, and those who benefit from gaining higher benefit for a lower percentage rate of taxation; the second faces the serious complication of 'ex post facto' exclusions for legislation, when dealing with Entitlements. This opposition can be negated, but the process produces further inequality.

The first step for Government is to abandon the claim Social Security is an Insurance program, underwritten by the beneficiaries. No Generation of beneficiaries in Social Security history has ever fully-funded their participation in the program. A clear statement Social Security is a Government-run welfare program subtracts the need to assert contributions arrive in the form of premiums. Payroll deductions can be classified as Tax, and tax can be modified freely to meet the needs of the program.

The first modification derivable from this change would be elimination of any limitation on contributions to the Fund. A percentage tax can be assessed on all Income, at all levels. There would be no maximum limit to the Tax. Higher Incomes would be made to pay their percentage share of the Tax. This would provide for the ability to lower the actual percentage rate, helping lower income classes; but do not look for this, considering the escalating costs of the program. The second advantage comes in the ability to deny benefits under the program, based upon magnitude of Income of Participant. This will immediately create great uproar!

Social Security was basically established to provide a subsistence program for people left with little income after Retirement. It was extended to provide for medical costs of people, who could not otherwise pay for them. Operation of the Social Security system has altered the modus operandi to underwrite the lifestyles of higher income classes, by providing them a substantive substitute income; which pays for their largest maintenance costs. Lower incomes are again left with inability to fund many of their pressing needs, even with a secondary income which is insufficient. All Incomes pay a much higher tax to fund the maintenance costs of the wealthier incomes, while finding their own maintenance costs increased without fully-funded cost structure.

Social Security must determine a level of minimum income necessary to sustain life in American society, and the equivalent level of medical premium payment annually to obtain Private insurance underwriting of Medicare guarantees. Legislation must be enacted by Congress stipulating no benefits will be granted to Incomes making more than 6.25 times the minimum level, which constitutes 16% of the total income. Medicare benefits will cease for Incomes in excess of 5.56 times the replacement premium level for medical insurance, equivalent to 18% of total income. Realize actual premium replacement levels for medical insurance will almost always be higher than yearly benefit income.

The legislation will have to be worded, so that it is a Tax; due to the Entitlements issue. There may also be need to 'Grandfather' present Participants in the program, because of widespread political opposition. The reality remains the Social Security program cannot withstand continuous addition of Beneficiaries, under current operation of total inclusion. The proposed alteration will cut beneficiaries by 45% from the Baby Boomer Generation. The long-run Savings to the general fund will be immense, with these Boomers expected to live an average thirty years past Retirement.

The remaining consideration must be the largesse of Social Security monthly benefits. Current beneficiaries will have to be 'Grandfathered', but new Retirees should be limited in benefits; to a level, which each is paid the annual minimum necessary income. The common monthly benefit will have economic benefits beyond general fund savings. It will provide positive pressure to equalize Rental rates, property tax rates, and Food and clothing pricing throughout the Country. It will present additional pressure to limit Prescription drug prices. It allows the Social Security administration greater leverage to limit Medicare cost payments. States will be pressured to provide Unemployment benefits, which conform to the minimum necessary income; but gain from lower welfare housing assistance costs. The Whole brings greater economic rationalization to the Welfare award system.

A short aside should be directed to the Negative Income Tax, as first proposed during the early 1960s, to replace Welfare assistance programs. All Plans proved to be somewhat unworkable, because of factors of replacement income insufficiency; and because of loss of work incentives. The Author believes Welfare Assistance should be continued, but a Work Incentive program should be implemented; one which would actually generate removal from the Welfare system.

The components of the Proposal are as follows:

1. Welfare support and Unemployment should be advanced as usual.

2. All Recipients should be allowed Part-time labor, until this Income equals 25% of benefits.

3. This additional Income can be exempted by an additional 10%, for each previous year of gainful employment of the Individual, including this Part-time labor; to a maximum of ten years.

4. This allows previous Workers to labor to 125% of their Welfare Assistance, before their benefits will be reduced on a dollar-for-dollar reduction rate.

5. The Proposal keeps welfare recipients actively looking for Jobs, allows those most in need of income—the long-term laborers—the ability to supplement their income, and eases the transition back into the Labor force.

11

The Straight or Flat Income Tax

The constant percentage Income Tax enjoys much favor among many Economists. The Author admits to an affection for the Flat tax. Troubles with this tax, though, make it's emplacement extremely doubtful. The constant percentage Income tax would be heavily regressive, if grafted onto the present forms of Income tax. Explanation comes only with exploration of the evolution of the Income tax.

The Head tax did not account at all for differences of Income among Taxpayers. The Income tax was born as consequence, where Income was taxed as percentage of total receipts. This also became unworkable, as the tax did not account for expense differences between Taxpayers; some spend multiples of others, to generate the same Income. Deductions and Exemptions were devised, to accommodate such added costs of operation. Tax credits came later, as incentives to added effort in the generation of Income. The basic structure of modern Income tax was created.

The basic structure, though, caused more involved debate; as inequities were still perceived. A constant percentage Income tax was observed to be regressive; the majority of the tax was paid by lower income classes, because of their greater numbers. Wealthier income classes enjoyed greater gain from the Economy, and greater protection of property and operation; than did the lower income classes, who had to support the government services to the wealthier incomes as part of their own gain from government services. Later it became a debate on whether it was viable for lower income classes to support their own welfare support services.

Great debate started on the Income issue, between Wealth Distribution and Wealth Concentration. Wealth Distribution basically stated Highs and Lows of Income distribution should be redistributed around a social Mean Income through setting of Tax rates; this process to maximize the standard of living for Everyone. The Wealth Concentration argument asserted this type of taxation would seriously cripple the necessary concentration of wealth for economic capitalization. The Debate started basically with the British Corn laws of the 1840s, and continue; the Wealth Distribution argument now suffering from fallacies of the 'Great Society' programs of the 1960s and 1970s.

The Wealth Concentration argument suffers from the dis-economies associated with excessive funding, derived from insufficient distribution of Profits. The dis-economies come from decreasing Profitability ratios for Investment, as insecure investments and capitalizations are entered into; all in efforts to forestall dispersals of Capital. This occurs not only from current Tax law, which insists on investment of Profits, to escape taxation; but Investor insistence on Dividends, if the funds are not absorbed by further investment. These decreasing Profitability ratios actually descend to the level of losses, where astute business organization and planning do not invest the funds.

The Wealth Distribution argument loses power because of reliance on historical argument, which relied on fallacies; and because of 'thinking inside the Box', where proposals are all based on the current tax structure. Their major error stands on insistence on excessive Income tax rates, based on progressive increments of percentage increase by level of Income. These excessive rates on higher incomes incite flight of income out of the Country, and the proliferation of Deductions, Exemptions, and Tax credits. The high tax percentage rates fuel the resistence to capital dispersals as dividends, as great amounts are destined to be lost to taxation.

The Flat Tax is not inherently regressive; it becomes regressive only through the operation of deductions, exemptions, and tax credits. The Personal Exemption is a perfect example: a $2500 personal exemption means great change in disposable income, to someone earning only $20,000 per year; much less to someone earning $100,000 per year. The expenditure pattern of the lower income is vitally affected by the award of the Personal Exemption, the higher income perhaps may dine out a little more. Sensible legislation would phase out the Personal Exemption by a certain percentage per $10,000, until it was zero at $70,000. This would be more generative of tax revenue, than raising the top progressive tax rates by 8.7% with the current system of deductions, in terms of real tax amounts collected.

Much work would have to be done to make a Flat tax progressive. The area of the work would have to be in restructuring the current Tax system. The Internal Revenue Service would have to provide an Average Income for Households of Four. The Average is used, instead of the Mean of these Households, to ensure there will always be sufficient funding for the Tax changes. Households of Four with this Average Income would get no Exemptions at all.

All Households below this Income would get $250 per $10,000 less of income than the Average Income, per dependent in the Household. All Households with Income higher than the Average Income, would be charged $250 per $10,000 above the Average Income, for each dependent in the Household. This would be straight subtraction from or addition to the simple percentage assessment of tax from Income; rationale for the additions lie in the added cost of government services generated by Dependents. Extra costs of dependents would be accounted in the context of less income for the Household, while the advantages of greater wealth would be taxed in the same context as government cost. The Accounting procedure is simple to accomplish, and equalization of Mean standards of living eased; lower incomes gaining tax advantage, with higher Incomes paying more equivalent share; all based upon membership share in the Economy.

Other Deductions, Exemptions, and Tax credits would be based on the same formula as the Personal Exemption. Medical deductions would be estimated on numbers of dependents per $10,000 segments below the Average Income for a Family of Four. Personal tax credits would be allowed under the same structure, applying pressure on lower incomes to invest; especially if they contain Households with many dependents. The actual dollar value of the base deduction can vary, to expand it's fullest usage; this usage advantageous throughout all incomes, the negative tax credit for higher incomes explained as tax revenue generation as investment commission tax. Full usage would actively alter the Saving ratio upward for below Average Incomes, and not appreciably alter investment patterns of higher incomes.

There is much economic literature describing the fact the Income tax leads Business to accumulate Debt, because Interest payments are deductible while Dividends are not. These Economists charge Corporations buy back their own Stock and Debt-finance as consequence. They claim Corporations should be allowed to deduct Dividend payments, to counteract this activity. The activity is real, but the Solution is fallacious. Interest payments should be altered to being only eighty percent deductible, Corporations paying as tax for the use of Capital; this tax designed to reduce Profits from Debt-financed operations by about half. This tax would reduce excessive Profits-taking by modern Corporate operations, produce viable tax revenue levels from Corporations—raising their dropping contributions, and increase dividend dispersals.

An economic rationalization of the system of deductions, Exemptions, and tax credits could both make a Flat tax viable, and equalize the standards of living in this Country. The essential element of this type program would be an actual reduction of the percentage rates which now are on the books. The real gain is high tax revenue at least economic duress for Taxpayers, with tax impact placed upon those with greatest ability to pay. Judicious use of the tax system would actually provide greater economic fuel, than does the current tax system.

12

The Progressive Income Tax

The previous Chapter gave rough analysis why the current system of deductions, exemptions, and tax credits destroyed a viable Flat-or constant percentage—Income tax. This system also ruined the durability of the Progressive Income Tax. The fundamental flaw comes in the Personal Exemption establishing a minimum income level, below which Tax is not paid. Once a minimum floor of Income is created, a network of special privilege exemptions follow; always reducing the total amounts of Income taxed.

The latest Bush Tax Plan allowed major Corporations with yearly Profits in the billions of dollars, to obtain Rebates for Income taxes which they had never paid in the first place. Supply-Side Economists asserts this was good for business, which it actually was not; but no matter, it was absolutely destructive of the Income tax. The tax system adopted the principle of a Negative Income Tax, but converted it to payments to the highest incomes in the World. Middle-range personal Taxpayers and Corporations see diversion of their taxes to basic Tax evaders, while they bear the cost of taxation. Tax evasion and pressure for special privileges expand in this milieu.

The Progressive Income Tax must be altered at the minimum, so it's application can be seen as universal by the taxed entities. Deductions, Exemptions, and tax credits should be allowed only in the form of Rebates, with the nominal tax always previously being paid. This serves the purpose of enforcing the rule that the Tax must be paid. It also places the Government ahead of the game; granting the Government the interim interest on the collections, rather than the Taxpayer; more likely result, a lower level of debt-service payments for the Government to pay.

Most Economist would protest the above change, claiming it would be an obstruction to economic performance. This is not the case! Business payments of the Tax reduces Paper Profits from financial instruments which have nothing to do with the productive process, eliminates almost half of experimental 'rush plunging' investments simply to avoid tax payments, and while it lower absolute total investment; it guarantees actual payment of the Tax, which doesn't happen half the time under the current regulations, due to convoluted Accounting procedures. The end-product of such alteration for business would be more carefully planned investment, which would still be fully-funded, and of higher profitability.

The full payment of Tax for personal taxpayers generates a forced Savings pattern among ordinary Labor; and some economic studies indicate lump-sum Rebates have been used by Blue Collar workers as principal means of financial instrument investment. Other studies express Consumers rationalize the economic choice of Consumption patterns to a great degree, when confronted with delays in final total Wage payments. Additional studies advise scarcity of partial income payments leads Consumers to study their priority needs, selecting most fulfilling Consumer product with greatest durability. This process allows Economic theorists to stipulate such Consumer activity generates the best distribution of production factors.

Another Income tax measure expressing great utility lies in the elimination of the distinction between Social Security taxes and Income taxes. The distinction gives the lower income classes an image they are escaping the payment of taxes; this is not true. It grants higher incomes classes desire to lobby for limitations of the Social Security tax. The Income tax law should be altered to stipulate a fundamental base sum of collected Income taxes go to the Social Security account of the Taxpayer. The sum should be set to establish conditions for a uniform monthly Social Security benefit for all. Insufficiency of collections for the Social Security base payment will lead to increases of base sum allotted, so higher incomes fund the uniform monthly benefit.

A fundamental condition for the above Plan must be the separation of the Medicare and Medicaid funds, from the general Social Security fund. The separation of the medical funds allows to an hourly charge for medical underwriting to be assessed on hours of work. This would be a sliding scale assessment, with the IRS announcing monthly the assessment rate to Employers. The practice generates immediate funding of all medical payments made by the Government, forestalling the underwriting of debt; and allows for a rationale planning of provision of medical payments for emergency services et al., for uninsured individuals in this Country.

Almost none of the above planning has viability, if Taxpayers are permitted front-end utilization of deduction, exemptions, and tax credits. The largesse of collections would not be present, while Rebate return for these items provide almost full payment of such limitations of Tax, in a manner beneficial to both Taxpayer and Government. Some economic estimates predict such collection procedures would actually increase legitimate revenue collection by fourteen percent, as tax evasion becomes more difficult. The collection of tax also provides for uniform setting of Rebate magnitudes, unlike the present granting or withholding of tax allowances by regional office.

The inherent destructive feature of every Progressive Income tax has always been the extreme rate differential between Income levels. One theoretical study visualized there should be no greater spread of rates than twenty-five percent, with a minimal tax on any Income of ten percent. Another economic study speculates there should be no greater spread than twelve percent between low and high rates of taxation; this based upon current system of tax exemptions. Most of these studies reflect the opinions of their own economic advocacy, rather than serious study of differentials, though the Author finds the 25% spread of tax rates the maximum spread; without great loss of revenue due to tax evasion.

One relatively understandable study has indicated no tax rate should ever exceed 44%, as greater rates actually bring reductions in revenue; this accounted by loss of incentive, evasion of taxes, and taxable Income flight. This places an upper limit to taxation, if the Study is to be believed; but does not present a realistic analysis for exact placement of rates. The Author will attempt to enter the fray, with probable laughter for all; after suggesting the 44% tax rate is too excessive, being destructive of short-term operating capitalization.

Arithmetic progression suggests used of the Bell Curve to determine tax rates. The lowest Ten percent of Incomes should pay the lowest rate, the highest ten percent of Incomes should pay the highest rate of tax. The Mean should pay twenty-two percent of tax, if 44% percent is deemed to be the highest rate of Tax. Placement on the Quadrant lines—halfway down the Bell curve on each side—should pay six percent less on the one side, and six percent more on the other. The lowest ten percent of the Curve should pay ten percent rate as tax; especially under the condition that Social Security taxes are integrated into the Income tax. This leaves the rates of 10%, 16%, 22%, 28%, and 44%. The Splits are determined by distance from the Mean on the Bell Curve, at 10% of Curve, quarter of Curve, three-quarter of Curve, and Ninety percent of Curve.

Most students of Taxes do claim there must be more incremental rate increases of the Tax, in interest of fairness; and to eliminate harsh impact upon the standard of living of low-end inhabitants of each segment. The Author accepts this analysis, but also understands the value of limited rate level changes. The basic rates could be halved once more, on the appropriate segment lines of the Bell Curve. He believes the system and the Taxpayer would be better served by utilization of the Personal Exemption formula of the last Chapter, along with the five rates of increase; as it would properly set weight between families and Individuals.

Economic students should realize Arithmetic progression, while seemingly fairer than other formulas; may not conform to the needs of Economics. Setting the Mean to pay the half-rate of maximum tax may or may not promote Consumer Demand or productivity. The Mean works excellently, if the distribution of Income matched the Bell Curve for Taxpayers. The Average Income can be to the left or right of the Mean Income. The schedule of rates may be shifted four percent to the right, if Average Income is four percent less than the Mean. Only the top two rates must be shifted to the left four percent, if Average Income is four percent more than the Mean. Neither case absolutely assures the proper economic matrix to advance performance.

A major detraction from efficient tax collection remains the classification of Income. The Author has always contended Income was Income, immaterial of from which it came. Personal Income, Capital Grains, Rents, Royalties, Business Income, Partnership Equity payments, and Corporate Income are all one and the same: Income. Classification splintering only allows for passage of special dispensations, most based on no economic factor. This curtails tax revenue collections, and thereby; increases the tax rates placed. The multiplicity of these tax exemptions grant inventive taxpayers the ability to evade most tax.

The Author once proposed the enactment of a tax law which would have simplified the tax code immensely. It simply stated each Taxpayer must fill out his own tax form, without help of any outside agent. The taxing agency was charged with insuring these tax forms were properly filled out and accurate. He contended taxing agencies would devise simplified forms in short order. He found such pressure on bureaucracies remained the sole means to eliminate idiocy of action. No support for such action can be found, as it would eliminate occupational positions in tax collection agencies; and Civil Service presents a formidable political lobby.

A more realistic approach to the problem may be passage of a Constitutional Amendment, which the Author will provide at the end of this Chapter. Such strictures may be the only method for the Public, by which they might limit the excess of political legislation; propelled by special interest lobbying. The intent of the Constitutional amendment does not hope or wish for an alteration of the conduct of Politics, in this or any other political system. It simply desires to limit the manner political interests are transmitted to the body politic. Here is the Constitutional amendment:

Congress will pass a Uniform Tax Code, without other tax legislation enacted into law; which shall not exceed twenty thousand words in length, and from which; all Federal revenues are to be collected. Any successive legislation must supplant and nullify any previous Tax Code, from which no tax collections can be made. All taxes imposed by the Federal Government must be stipulated in the Code, else they are null and void.

[Some may wonder why the necessity for the Constitutional amendment. The limitation of physical wording size cancels any political attempts to hide chicanery in the midst of verbosity. Tax law must be clearly outlined, definite in wording and intent, and serve as the basis for taxing agency regulation; all of which must conform to the legislation. Politicians must include the specific legislative intent to raise Federal revenues, leaving little room to dispense political patronage. The physical construct is sufficient to write effective legislation covering several means of taxation, while leaving a traceable form which can be analyzed by All; who are concerned with unfair or discriminatory taxing.]

13
Tax Theory

Tax theory runs rampant through all forms of business literature, political literature, Economic literature, Newspapers, periodicals, and TV shows. Political pundits spend at least five percent of their time in discussion of various proposed tax legislation. Tax affects the greatest majority of people, and in an adverse way. Everyone has an opinion about Taxes, almost all contending tax assessments are too large. It is a thing Most would like to be rid of, and many try evasive means to be rid of it.

Tax theory must consider the elements of Taxes, else discussion stands as useless; just venting animosity. The necessary elements of Taxation can be simply listed:

1. Taxes must provide the revenue for government services.

2. They need be placed upon those with ability to pay, or revenues will not be gained;

3. They must uniformly impact all subject to tax

4. They should not discriminate between Taxpayers

5. They should not unduly restrict economic performance.

This seems like a simple list, quite straightforward; but actual simplicity ends with the list. Every element on the list is commonly violated, even in the United States; where there is sharp allegiance, at least in vocalization, for tax equalization. Each of the conditions will be studied for clarification.

Taxes in this Country most often do not pay for government services, only for Debt service; which Debt actually pays for those Government services. The George W. Bush administration took office with deliberate Tax Plan, goal of said Plan was to stop repayment of Federal Debt; through curtailment of the Government surplus of tax revenues. The effective fact that the surplus had already disappeared, did not detract them from the Bush Tax Cut; the payoff to his Corporate political support. The resulting deficit spending is dismissed as necessary operating expenses for a War on Terrorism and Iraq, both wars where only they can perceive conclusive Enemy agents. Truth demands statement the Federal budget would have run deficit, even without September 11th, or Saddam Hussein.

Internal Defense Dept. estimates vary, but general consensus states War with Iraq will be expensive—the Author estimates 120 billion dollars if it is a short war. This sum is not integrated in the purported current Federal deficit, though large sums are already being spent in preparation. These preparations are being conducted under the Bush Tax Cut, where Corporations do not pay tax on the profits of these preparations, and are effectively allowed to set their own prices for supplied items.

The above discussion is not a denunciation of the Bush administration per sec, as the process do not vary much from the traditional American preparations for war. American business has always viewed Wars as proper conduit for Profits-taking. They always insist on deficit-spending for such Wars, so as not to be distracted by taxes on their Profits. This has been the unilateral policy without exception, since the War of Jenkins' Ear. American business remain highly resistant to tax rates which could pay off Government debt, whether it is Federal, State, or Local; maintaining it adversely affects the Economy.

The placement of tax upon those with ability to pay si highly subject to interpretation. Higher income classes exercise tax regulations to limit their taxation. The Author estimates the majority of Households of Four making $100,000 per year pay less than the average payment made by Households of Four making $40,000 per year. He goes on to estimate approximately twelve percent of Household debt of the lesser income directly derives from the higher income Household not paying the properly multiplied payment of taxes. This outcome determined by increased taxes, higher Interest rates on Consumer Credit and Mortgages, and the production of a higher Inflation rate.

Mention of the adverse impact of the Sales tax upon lower incomes has been outlined in a previous chapter. The total restrictive nature of the Sales tax may not be realized. The largesse of the Sales tax revenues collected from lower income classes, realistically replaces the Income tax which they no longer pay. The magnitude is approximately the same dollar values; but wait, did We not say the Social Security tax had replaced the Income tax? Could this mean that the real, or actual tax rate imposed, has actually doubled for these lower incomes? This in an economic ecology where the actual tax rate of higher incomes, the amounts they really pay; has halved since the Reagan administration; when considered as percentage of amount to Income.

The Author asserts pro-actively the increasing Consumer debt throughout the Economy, with concentration in the lower income classes; simply portrays the exact unpaid taxes of the higher income classes, since the Reagan administration. The Author makes this assertion because of his belief lower income levels could not endure added taxation without loss of standards of living, or substitute debt capitalization of their lives. The withdrawn taxes had to be funded by deficit spending or tax collections from lower incomes, bringing accumulation of Consumer debt.

The Consumer debt is simply rolled forward, like Federal debt rollover. The Author realistically acknowledged lower income classes work themselves out of debt, and begin to accumulate a Capital base; though this process takes an estimated decade of dedicated effort. The maintenance of Consumer debt levels with growth, only reflects the subjection of new, youthful labor cadres to the excessive debt. New Households fund the tax credits to the Rich, with additional gains of profitability by funding of Consumer Credit.

The ability to pay taxes can be highly distorted, by provision of eased Consumer credit, and extension of tax dispensations to higher income classes. Lower incomes classes get to fund the tax evasion of higher income classes, through their desire to maintain their lifestyle. This effort is encouraged and advertised by Business, in the name of higher Profits. The Author realizes there is doubt of this assessment, but numbers back the assertion; the startup costs for beginning Households are huge, and can no longer be financed by Income alone-even two Incomes; this analysis does not include basic normal Mortgage debt, common to all households.

The current system of taxation clearly does not impact upon all equally, with the number and kind of tax credits, exemptions, and deductions granting wealthier incomes immunity from tax impact; necessitating only the employment of Accountants knowledgeable of the regulations of the tax code. Ordinary Accounting agencies employed by median-income classes, like H&R Block and other tax-Preparers, find tax agencies denying their common use of deductions, exemptions, and tax credits; all commonly granted to tax-preparers who cater to higher income classes. Tax agencies deny these tax reductions because they know median income Taxpayers will not fund the legal costs of Contest of tax agency rulings. There is inequality of tax placement. The above is direct discrimination between Taxpayers, based solely on ability to pay the extreme legal costs involved, of defense of their rights under the tax code. This is not subject to just the ability to pay, as median income Taxpayers consider all legal costs would be borne by themselves with loss of tax case in Court, and Rebate of taxes would only marginally exceed the legal costs, if at all;

under condition of winning the Court case. Tax agencies utilize such considerations to place tax burden in a discriminatory manner.

Consideration of the impact of the current tax system on economic performance express high levels of dis-economies. The average Sales taxes assessed magnify under conditions of Consumer credit. The Sales taxes are financed along with the purchase price of the Good, under Consumer credit. This increases the total debt by an average of 8%, raising the final cost of the Sales tax to the Consumer a probable two percent, before repayment of the Consumer loan is completely made; thereby, raising the tax impact to ten percent to Consumers using Consumer credit. More than half of all Taxpayers use Consumer credit for better than thirty percent of their purchases. Different expression of the cost could state Sales tax impact is greater than Income tax impact, for at least the lowest two-fifths of Income classes.

The Sales tax impact increases the use of consumer credit by a multiple of it's actual percentage rate with Interest, so the expansion of Consumer credit must be attributed to be almost fifteen percent; all due to the Sales tax. The use of consumer credit magnified the product price to the Consumer by an average of 1.3 times with running Credit balances, so Consumers who use consumer credit can be estimated to pay almost 18–20% more for their overall purchases; all directly connected to Sales tax impact.

The Sales tax system in use restricts Consumer Demand by at least the above stated amount, and probably lowers the standard of living for those who use Consumer credit, by approximately five percent overall. The cost of this detriment comes from combination of Sales tax and debt finance. This is direct loss of Consumption by at least half of Taxpayers. One must listen to the counter-argument, which states at least half of this loss would still be realized by alternate forms of taxation; but this still leaves about a two percent loss in the standard of living from the current Sales tax, for about half of the Population in this Country; this loss over and above the direct reduction of Consumption by Sales tax rate.

The impact of the Income tax, with it's current riddle of tax reductions, is harder to access to damage to economic performance. Tentative economic studies (speculative) suggest it is eight times harder for an Income less than $50,000 to invest a dollar, than for an Income over $80,000 to invest a dollar. This clearly indicates there is a plateau of Income past which life maintenance costs do not intervene in Investment decisions. Most Economists suggest this plateau may be reached when Income arrives above $30,000, but transference to ease of Investment is slow; all because of non-economic decisions of Consumption.

The Author finds Income tax impact has more to do with the delayed ease of Investment, than does non-economic decisions of Consumption (upgrades of Housing, cars, etc.) Common vehicles of Investment—IRAs etc.—rarely are able to exercise the discounts granted to Investment under the Income tax code, all due to required magnitudes of Investment to qualify, or stipulations on unitary investment, rather than investment spread (for security purposes). Workers investing through Payrolls deductions to a retirement fund, rarely can manipulate the $10,000 transactions; for the purpose of qualifying for advanced tax credits. This does not impact seriously on the level of Investment, but does discriminate against smaller Investors; and does retard the accumulation of capital assets by lower income classes.

Actual economic performance is not seriously damaged, except for slower capital accumulation by lower income Households; as the level of Investment could only be expected to rise marginally under equal tax conditions. It does lengthen the period of time it takes for households to reach fully-financed economic viability; but does not alter significantly the Consumption patterns of households with minimum incomes of $35,000 per year. The current Income tax system limits adverse economic impact caused by discrimination of tax regulation against lower income households.

Reasons for this discrimination result from a variety of factors. The first and foremost is desire of higher income households to evade taxes, by having lower income households bear the greatest amount of the tax burden. The second major reason is the financial profits gained by the Consumer credit industry, who finds a overall quarter increase in the use of Consumer credit from use of the current Income tax code. The third major cause lies in the desire of Business for Labor to use the tax-deductible retirement funds, which increase stock values while eliminating effective Stockholder interference with Management through diffusion of Fund control; the current Income tax code carefully crafted to insure almost total use of such tax-deductible funds. A fourth reason states the Income tax code allows Corporate managements to guide the Investment decisions of the majority of funds invested, through channelization of the Investment—a type of Investment scheduling set up to fund capitalization schedules.

The tax system of this Country was clearly sculpted for many reasons beyond effective funding of government services. This process expressly extends beyond expression of Government economic policy, as many of the taxes imposed actually reduce economic performance. Much of the tax code reflects special interests' desires to fund and bring profitability to the Consumer credit industry. Many elements of the tax code pressure to directed levels of Investment, which does not challenge current Corporate leadership; and fund capital investment schedules developed by this leadership. The Whole is directed towards lower income households bearing the greatest burden of the actual, real tax burden; these households effectively paying eighty percent of the actual taxes, though higher income households hold eighty percent of the capital assets, and make seventy percent of the total income.

The remaining chapters of this work will examine alternative, speculative forms of taxation. These have been derived by the Author, though he draws from the efforts of others. The Author does not claim exclusive right to these explicated forms, and requests excuse; if he in any way nullifies recognition to others.

14

The One-Tax System

Economists of old often considered the imposition of one tax, as converse a multiplicity of taxes. They argued the singular tax upon all would provide ease of tax collection, and due to the sole source of government revenue; be designed to generate the necessary revenues in the most viable economic method. The Counter-argument stated such a singular tax would be inherently unfair, as no methodology could be devised to accommodate all economic positions and structures; and would lead immediately to effective tax evasion techniques, with reductions in generated revenues. The Author agrees with both arguments; yet, finds the singular tax of amazing interest, believing the fewest assessed forms of tax to be best in terms of economic performance and fairness.

He suggested, IN SEARCH OF THE PERFECT ECONOMIC MATRIX (iUniverse, 2002), a whole number of tax classifications should be eliminated; with the substitution of a One-Tax Income system. He proposed the integration of Corporate Income tax, Personal Income tax, Capital Gains tax, Business Income tax, Partnership Share taxes, Royalties, Commercial Rents tax, and most Excise taxes inside a simple proscribed Income tax. Financial gain from any venue was to be considered Income, no matter how derived, and no matter who derived the financial generation. Wages, Profits, Royalties, Rents, Dividends, and Interest would not be sorted by manner of generation; with no allowances made for the activity involved.

The Author acknowledges the need to reduce total Income by the expenditures required to generate the Income, to be considered as Cost expenses. These would be allowed to all forms of Income. Business could deduct their normal expenses, Dividend income could deduct paperwork and commission costs, Authors could deduct an hourly life maintenance wage. Royalties and Commercial Rents could deduct capitalization costs etc. Personal Wages could even be allowed an hourly life maintenance cost, rather than a unit Personal Exemption; likewise, the same schedule for Dependents. These Costs expenses could be specified or classed for normal deduction from the Income tax.

The entire system of current deductions, exemptions, and tax credits would be eliminated. They would either not be replaced, or more economically rational substitutions would be made. Business would lose the entire tax credit and investment credit allowances, substituted with the greater Social desire of deductions for each employee hired full-time; with substitution of total numbers of Labor hours employed, for those using Part-time labor. Investors would be granted a one-tax credit for Investment of specified amount, like the current Personal Exemption; under provision Taxpayers have invested at least twice the financial size of the tax credit; the Author suggest something less than $5000.

Inherent to the success of such a tax would be demand taxes be paid, upon receipt of the Income; no delays being allowed in any case. This nullifies the efforts of current Accounting procedures, all designed to delay reportage of taxable income for as long as possible; for the effective utilization of the income in the interim before taxation. Most would protest this limitation; the Author only need state current tax receipts in the current tax system would double, if immediate declaration of taxable revenues was demanded. The practice raises the tax burden for all, while not appreciably increasing the wealth of the Practitioners; operating costs of the practice leaving only about twenty percent profit on the actual amount of taxes defrayed.

Most Economists and all Business personnel will claim a limited Investment tax credit adversely affects total investment and Savings ratios. The claim will be untrue! Business makes it's Profits through utilization of Capital; they would not alter their procedures because of a loss of percentage tax credits for Investment. Investors make the choice between Consumption and Investment, which is little affected past a certain maximum level of Consumption. The set limit tax credit for Investment would actually incite lower income households to save and invest more, to meet the conditions for the tax credit for Investment, if there were multiple set Investment tax credits to entice all income levels. Higher income households and Business would get a like, limited tax credit; but would not be paid for what they will do anyway, at detriment to all Taxpayers.

The consideration of whether such a One-Tax should be Progressive, or a Flat percentage, need be discussed. The Flat percentage tax truly discriminates against the lowest incomes, who are induced to pay the same rate as those much better off; in economic terms, with a much greater ease of tax payment. Median income Taxpayers claim they should gain some tax break, because they do not make quite as much as their Peers. The higher incomes scream progressive taxes are nothing but Wealth Distribution schemes which destroy the economic incentives of productive activity. The Author contends the Poor need a break, the median incomes demand a tax-inspired non-economic advantage, and the Rich are just plain greedy with no viability to their argument.

There should be a three-tier system of Progressive tax; with the lowest Percentile quarter of Incomes paying a tax rate of twelve percent, the highest percentile quarter of Incomes paying a tax rate of 35%, while the two middle quarters pay a tax rate of 22% (notice this is different than a straight Bell Curve analysis, which the Author regards as economically disadvantageous). The lowest income households are protected by the life maintenance deductions from excess taxation, the transition to median income can be cushioned by use of the investment tax credit, the median incomes will be induced to work harder and save more, and the higher incomes enjoy freedom of investment without extreme rates of taxation.

Life maintenance deductions would be estimated differently than the current system, somewhat outlined earlier. These deductions will be based upon number of hours worked, with an average 40-hour Workweek granted to Anyone; who cannot prove greater numbers of hours worked. This deductions would be standard and constant for Everyone, and based solely upon the costs of life maintenance common in American society; all determined by minimum Rent charge, daily minimum food costs, fuel, clothing, and transportation costs by cheapest means. The Author would advocate $2.70 per hour for life maintenance, plus $1.40 per hour per Dependent. Nc one would be granted more than 260 hours per month. The resultant reductions in tax would equate effectively with actual living costs; and would be subtracted from Income before tax rate was assessed for all. It equates with Dependents to an equivalence with the Minimum Wages, which does not call for Minimum Wage increases; but leaves little to tax at this level.

Social Security contributions would be integrated into the Income tax system, so lower incomes would mainly be paying for their own retirement programs. A set limit of tax would be allocated for each taxpayer, and transferred to his Social Security account. The set limit determined by the total level necessary for current year payment of all Social Security dispersions, so higher incomes would contribute to lower income deficiencies. The Social Security administration would still account for individual payments (though higher incomes would pay unfulfilled Account payments), but this system allows for eventual transfer to a One-Benefit system for Social Security; a necessity which have previously been discussed.

Business and Corporate income would be considered no differently than personal forms of income, but would gain deduction for the amounts of labor they employ. This deduction for employees should be equal to the deduction given to ordinary taxpayers for dependents. Like ordinary taxpayers citing major expenses for dependents, even when such dependents have independent income; Business can cite their capitalization expenses for employment of labor. They would also be held to the same limit tax credit for Investment, as ordinary taxpayers; but they would get special dispensation for use of Investment credit for each employee (2080 hours of labor per year), due to the largesse of the capitalization for employment. This union of all taxpayers eliminates special dispensations for differentiated classes of taxpayers. All would be united in resistence to usurious exercise of taxing, by Governmental agencies.

The above argument brings up need for determination of the limited tax credit for Investment. The Author believes the tax credit of definite limit should be tiered, to provide some ease of investment for lower incomes. He proposes:

1. a $250 tax credit, for investments of $1000

2. a $1000 tax credit, for investments of $5000

3. a $10,000 tax credit, for investments of $100,000 and up.

(Tax credits in this instance, are described as direct reductions of the final tax bill to the taxpayer, after all legitimate expenses has been allocated from the tax base.)

The individual taxpayer would be allowed an additional tax credit for each dependent, when the investment is separated from the ownership of the taxpayer in the dependent's name; though parents can retain control of the funds, until the dependent reaches legal maturity. This places the individual taxpayer on the same plane as the Business organization.

Legitimate business expenses must also be looked into, if proper apportionment of tax be placed. The Author once proposed Business not be allowed deduction of management costs and advertising costs, as these are expenses of the organization which are not productive costs per sec. This, though, stands as relatively harsh; also restrictive of business alignment and trade. This does not deny excesses expressed in the area, utilized by businesses to cancel debt. Rationalization of the process must take place.

A limitation on advertising costs would benefit the Consumer, postal services, and the wages of employees; who are shorted by excess expenditure on advertising. The enactment of the tax should legally limit advertising expense deduction to twelve percent of the value of the product. This is to be determined by the total Wholesale price of the total numbers of units of the product sold. Both Manufacturers and Retailers would be allowed this advertising expense, so the actual deduction would be a potential 24% of the total price of the products. Expenditures on advertising above this limit could be made, but would not be deductible from final tax.

Much critique of excessive Management salaries exists, because of the exponential increase in such salaries and benefits, since the Reagan administration. The quandary can be settled by simple taxation, which the Author will jokingly call the Lux rule:

> The Tax law shall stipulate normal business organization should be set up as a 12-tier Wage system; such separate levels providing distinguishment for differences of training and skill. Business shall be able to deduct total allocations for Labor in any form, except medical insurance of labor; only to a ratio of twelve times the lowest yearly income of any employed.

The wealthier incomes will immediately declare this is a Wealth distribution plan, and it is. The beauty of it lies in the pressure it applies to maintain a standard of living for the lower Wage levels, and the restriction on excessive Consumption by the better-paid Wage levels. The Plan does not disallow remuneration above these limits, only tax deductions for such payments. This exclusion from deduction from the tax base, includes all forms of return: salaries, paid-up Life insurance, annuities, stock options, and retirement plans which exceed those of the lowest Wage earners. Company loans to Employees must be made through a Company Credit Union, and must demand the same Interest rates for all Employees; rates determined by risk to capital involved, with funding for Stock Options disallowed.

Economists have lately derided Wealth distribution tax plans, accounting them to economically inefficient. Their basic argument consists of statement such plans artificially alter the incentive program of the market system. This argument becomes a basic lie, when elements of the leadership use social union to demand remuneration; at levels higher than their own contribution to the productive process. Corporate and Business executives Today, use the dispersion of Stock ownership, and common remuneration packages; to insist they deserve such levels of payment; though their contributions to the productive process is often detrimental and generate loss of Profits.

Economic argument for some measure of Wealth distribution stands as it is a support of proper Consumer Demand, which generates a level of Consumption; that maximizes capitalization of product production. It serves as a direct expansion of the Consumer population, through provision of Consumption dollars at proper alignment, for maximization of Product Sales. Wealth distribution schemes which operate off welfare dispersals do significantly alter economic incentives in the economy; but a tax system pressuring for a fair distribution of Wage does not impact the incentives of the economy.

Income taxes currently enjoy favor among Economists, as the principle means of revenue collection for government services. The Author does not disagree with them to any great degree; understanding tax collections of whatever form, possess reductions for the economic productive process. Most Economists do not evaluate the potential loss to economic performance, by such lack of provision of government services; which, in themselves, are incentive to economic productivity. Income taxes are simply considered a necessary evil, and their examination does not extend past this point. The system of Income taxation, though, is not immutable. The idea there must be an Income tax is not true, or effective in the consideration of viable economic taxing systems. Other forms of tax systems can be devised, and studied for potential impact. The rest of this book will be a theoretical exploration of forms of taxation, with consideration of possible economic impacts of such taxes.

15

The Bank Deposit Tax

The Author first discussed this form of tax in PLANS FOR THE FUTURE (Xlibris, 2000). The Bank Deposit Tax would simply set a percentage tax upon deposits into financial institutions, with a yearly additional assessment made upon any deposit or financial instrument untouched for a year. This would be a Flat income tax without consideration of any expenses of the taxpayer. The rate, though, would be so low as to equate with a Sales tax; the Author proposed two percent. The nature of this tax has many benefits which discount both the hazards of Sales taxes, and the non-recognition of ability to pay.

The Bank Deposit tax is a misnomer, as it would apply to all financial institutions and instruments. All would be subject tax, including Credit Card companies; but this would be a tax upon their income, not Consumers. The tax ignores Cash transactions, defining them as irrelevant; as all income flows through financial institutions at some point, necessary for funding productive functions. All Market transactions will eventually be subject to tax, though delays of up to a year may be incurred.

The reach of the tax is all-inclusive, so Investment is taxed as well as Consumption. The tax, though, is an in-process tax; where the tax is assessed at every step of the production and consumption cycle. It is a tax upon Income, not Consumption; so Investment is not favored over Consumption. Investors are charged equally with Consumers, so capitalization costs will rise; but with only a flat increase of no great magnitude. Higher income classes pay the same rate as lower income classes, but pay a much higher numeral level of tax; due to their greater participation in the Economy.

The greatest benefit of the Bank Deposit tax comes in the level of governmental revenues raised by the tax. All economic Participants are taxed equally, at the point of their basic participation. The charge is not excessive, so leaves the littlest economic impact of collection; as any of the tax systems currently in place. It can provide a high degree of liquidity with minute reductions of the tax rate, though, for stimulation of the economy; a percentage point reduction can free both Investment and Consumption dollars to the economy, making it a fine instrument for Government interaction in the economy for stimulus or suppression of inflationary pressures.

The collection process remains quite simple for taxing agencies, needing only to supervise financial institutions, who provide daily collections through computer program; with relatively no avenue for tax evasion. This daily collection process would potentially reduce debt service costs for Government, by a possible eight percent of current costs. The overall costs to the Government of tax collections could reduce by three-quarters of the current expense. Collections, tax registration and payments, and expenses would all be speeded and improved.

Tax revenues from the Bank Deposit tax would reduce under recessive economic conditions, but not as greatly as other current tax systems; unless Government economic policy thought to stimulate the economy by rate reductions. This rate reduction stimulus under such recessive conditions, would spur the economy at all levels: reducing resource pricing, production and distribution costs, Retail costs, and increasing Consumer income. The tax serves as an excellent vehicle for economic stimulus, or for Inflation retardant.

It is obvious such a Bank Deposit tax could easily replace the Income tax system. The Flat rate would insure all paid tax, the in-line collection of the tax determines the level of taxes paid depended upon the level of participation within the economy. There would be absolute equality of tax, based upon participation.

The impact of Foreign trade would have to be integrated into the tax system, so all funds transferred out of the Country would have the tax applied. This assures no favoritism will be shown to foreign products in American markets, and Americans could not shift their profits from participation in the economy overseas, to evade the tax. Foreign business and product would endure not tariff, or other discrimination; and such foreign entities could adjust their prices to nullify the tax impact.

One of the great values of the Bank Deposit tax lies in the lack of Accounting difficulties associated with the tax system. All business organizations can easily determine the price increases necessary, to maintain the profitability of their operations in the face of taxation. Markups to displace profit losses are determined by straight percentage, without extraordinary evaluations about tax credits, deductions, or exemptions. A whole range of Accounting procedures can be discarded as unnecessary, with the known flat percentage rate imposed.

The economic advantages of the Bank Deposit tax may not be clearly seen. Individuals do not need be supervised for tax reportage or collection. Accounting procedures are reduced to a minimum, while the degree of tax evasion reduces to practically zero. Financial institutions and instruments alter their rates of return to reflect the tax impact upon those deposit arrangements. Foreign products or components must pay their fair share of tax, in order to participate in the American economy. Higher income classes pay a greater amount of tax, due solely to their own participation in the economy.

The Bank Deposit tax has other economic advantages. It enjoys the lack of impact along with Sales taxes; but it generates much higher revenues, and does not discriminate against Consumption. It provides easy stimulus to the economy, by Government economic action. It provides equal taxation to Investment and Consumption, so actually giving stimulus to Investment; the tax system eliminates lump-sum payments to the Government, now providing a substitution effect for investments. Savings are greatly facilitated, as taxation can be integrated in normal household expense.

Such a tax would be integrated into the price scheduling system of this Country, and thereby serve as a retardant to Inflation. Producers and Retailers would hesitate to increase prices, due to the potential loss of Sales; of much greater effect when dealing with both business and Consumers. Business decision-making and loan extension, on the other hand, require less contemplation; due to elimination of tax accounting considerations. The tax becomes a simple production cost for business, which can be easily scheduled.

The specific effects of the Bank Deposit tax on the economy must be examined. Middleman costs would undoubtedly diminish, as both Producers and Retailers sought to eliminate a level of taxation, to increase Profits and reduce loss of Sales from pricing. Producers would expand into Distribution of their own product, attaining the Profits of the distribution process. Retailers would develop extended purchasing programs, saving on exterior commission costs. Actual employment rolls may go up, as Middlemen organizations traditionally utilize minimal staffing of low pay, little medical or retirement benefits, and poor training.

Consumer prices may actually decrease through impact of the tax, because of elimination of Middleman costs. This should be negated by a percentage increase of Consumer credit costs, but applies greater pressure to Save and invest, truly heightened by elimination of lump-sum tax payments. Restriction from Consumption by tax regulation should be removed from the Consumption patterns of higher income classes, as evasion of tax cannot be attained. This would lead to heavier Consumption among higher income classes, offsetting reduction of lower income Consumption from higher Consumer credit charges. The Author estimates a seven percent potential increase in actual Consumption in dollars; equivalent to a 700,000 jobs increase.

The impact upon financial institution must be considered. Elimination of lump-sum tax payments should actually increase their net Reserves by nine percent, though many Economists would disagree with this estimate. Consumer credit should actually decrease by about six percent, as Consumer acquired ease of Savings through elimination of Income taxes, and the Bank deposit tax forced increase in Consumer credit rates. Business, though, would likely transfer nine percent of their capitalization to exterior sourcing; making bank assets a premium commodity, possibly increasing Interest rates. Financial institutions would probably profit by a transfer to a Bank Deposit tax.

Production could actually increase, as Profit margins thinned because of an additional production cost. This would incite additional production in business enterprise which were not on full production. This would further pressure for self-distribution, for a better Wholesale price schedule. Retailers would finds themselves receiving a better over-all Wholesale price schedule for products, and face increased resistence to heavy Retail markups, in order to maximize Sales. Consumers would realize higher income levels for Savings, along with less debt-finance charges.

Economists will contest the Author presents too rosy a picture of the advantages of the Bank Deposit tax. He sidesteps the charge, by claiming the inherent economic factors are there; how they would finally operate will always be open to debate. He continues to assert alternatives to Income tax does exist, and in forms which could be more beneficial than the current system. The importance of this tax lies in the spread impact of the tax upon the economy, equating effectively with a normal production cost. The withdrawal of sharp tax impact would, in itself, be an economic performance incentive; of what magnitude need be evaluated.

[Economic students must learn to think outside the Box. Every Economy is a complex weave of interrelationships, on the order of a Chinese puzzle; but one which can be put together in numerous different ways. The search for the perfect fit remains the goal of the Economist, and

one which will never be found; as Economies evolve under growth.
The search retains a scent of unrequited love.]

16

The Wholesale Tax

This tax thinks to give Government the residual benefits of enterprise. It required a percentage tax on Wholesale goods, with like tax on imported goods; so the Government derives an entrepreneurial profit off of production. It operates as an economic profit paid to the Government, with all the hazards of economic profits. The fundamental result is a double charge of profit-taking from production costing.

Most Economists may doubt the claim of double-charge of profits, but study of such tax placement does suggest derived revenues would not be of high magnitude; without introduction of a high percentage rate. The Wholesale tax differs from Excise taxes, in the fact it is a percentage tax; rather than a per unit tax. It functions over the entire range of Wholesale products, unlike Excise taxes; demands per unit charges be low, to maintain economic performance. Excise taxes can often double, or triple, the per unit cost of the product; both gaining high revenue, and limited to products of intense demand. The percentage tax cannot do this, and revenues remain lower than Sales taxes; unless the percentage rate equates with business profits.

The extraction of revenue in taxation at the Wholesale product stage has serious adverse economic effects. The required percentage rate for the production of sufficient revenue will seriously pressure for less than full normal production cost entrepreneurial profit. This will reduce Investment capital for production, because of reduced rates of return. The pressure is extended rearward, and capitalization of resource-recovery is impaired. Wages throughout the production process are poorly stabilized, with elimination of pay-raises for increased production or proficiency. The entire production process starts to starve for funds.

The exact placement of the tax extraction also brings on a normal Retail profits charge for the magnitude of the tax extraction, over and above the normal markup for retail services. This will introduce a product price structure, artificially raised by not only the percentage of the wholesale tax; but also by a normal profit on the tax. The impact of the wholesale tax thereby produces almost direct reduction in Consumption; suppressing production below the actual tax extraction.

This reduction of production is magnified by the stratification of Wages in the production and resource-recovery sectors. Theoretical economic models tentatively indicate the actual loss of Consumption and Production can be more than twice the total extraction of the total revenues of the wholesale tax. Add in the loss of return for capitalization of the production and resource-recovery sectors, and Investment can reduce to less than a quarter of it's normal spread before introduction of the wholesale tax.

Some Economists have long speculated on the conditions of a stable, long-termed deflationary period. Almost every instance of short-term deflation quickly drops into economic recession. The percentage Wholesale tax could possibly possess the foundation to provide for a stable long-term deflationary period, but the Author speculates the percentage rate would have to remain less than 6.5% in order to avoid recession; and government services likely could not be maintained with this level of tax revenue generation. Any attempt would probably descend into economic recession.

The Wholesale tax also suffers from extreme Collection costs. It remains an intricate system of tax collection, greater than personal Income tax; because of the magnitude of products to be taxed. This becomes worsened by the spread of products throughout the Economy. No one tax supervisor can oversee one product, as it is distributed throughout the Country. Simple supervision at production source is impossible, because of foreign imports. Multiplicity of production sites compound the situation, as supervision at source must be maintained; with actual supervision at distribution for assessment of tax. Almost half of tax revenues would be eaten by collection costs.

The Wholesale tax system also suffers from major tax evasion costs. The Author implies almost eight percent of the wholesale tax could be lost simply to oversight. Actual tax evasion cost might exceed one-third of total revenues collected; pressuring for increase of percentage rate of tax. Tax evasion contains little risk, as denial capacity has great ease; claims of losing manifests relatively easy. Manifest check must locate product load, point of delivery, and original production site; before a tax claim against product can be made by taxing agent.

Long-term economic consequences of the Wholesale percentage tax consist of undercapitalization of resource-recovery and production sectors, reduction of Capital Gains, reduction of actual Production and Consumption levels, and stratified personal incomes. Revenues will not be sufficient from such a tax to pay for government services over extended implementation of the wholesale tax, and will generate either government debt, or further taxation. Extended use of the wholesale tax assures recessionary conditions, whether sharp or lingering under-productivity. Inflation will impact with accumulation of government debt under such conditions; creating an economic milieu equivalent to the late 1970s–early 1980s.

17

The Retail Tax

The percentage Retail tax stands as a more realistic tax than the Wholesale tax, though it also has many disadvantages. The Retail is a percentage tax upon the markup for Retail services. This is a tax which places full cost of taxation on the Consumer, like Sales taxes. It squeezes the Retail sector, cutting Retail profits and Wages. The Consumer pays much higher prices for products, than even under heavy Sales tax, equivalent to Added-Value taxation. The Production process is left relatively untaxed.

The Retail tax also has major problems of tax collection and tax evasion. A major problem under Retail taxation comes from registration of business as Retail establishments. Mail-order houses proliferate under the Retail tax, most of which go unregistered until caught. This is direct tax evasion, but extremely profitable to both entrepreneur and Consumer. Stopping this medium of tax evasion requires huge expenditure, locating and closing such tax discount houses; especially under an online Internet ordering system. Extended use of the Retail tax will bring a twenty percent evasion of the tax burden, through such venues.

There is a direct reduction of Consumption from a Retail tax, reducing Consumer Demand; but not impacting the Production process. A fairly immediate and constant economic effect becomes reduction of the Production process labor force. This leads to escalating reductions in Consumer Demand, with loss of Consumption. The tax on Consumption leaves the Production process alone, but has many effects on it.

Reduced Consumption rates bring immediate reductions in production levels, but has left the Production process untaxed. This lack of taxation leads production facilities to raise product prices, to replace profits lost in lack of Sales; Inflation will immediately begin to flourish. The same effect could be observed in the period 1978–1990, where personal income taxes remained high; but business taxes were vastly reduced.

Consumption shrank per household, though increases in employment curtailed extenuated Consumption losses during the Period; though the Unemployment rate remained high. Huge increases in Investment were made, in the face of under-Consumption; simply due to the penalty of Consumption, and the advantage of Investment. Capital returns proved inadequate, because of the lack of Consumption. Financial institutions began to suffer, as they could not achieve a viable rate of return for the increased deposits they received. Resource-recovery and production sectors became over-capitalized, as was Retail and Housing; all due to the lack of tax restraint upon the production process.

The Retail percentage tax would incite like conditions to the Period cited above, except Consumption rates would decrease faster; without the aid of increasing employment, Investment capitalization construction employment would not absorb labor losses in the Production sector. The rate of Capital return would drop more rapidly, with financial institutions issuing Paper with below-scale Interest rates for profitability. Most tax systems impacting upon the Consumer will in the long-term produce reductions in Employment, producing decelerating Consumption.

The actual revenues gained for government services will be insufficient, so further taxation becomes necessary. Increasing the percentage rate of Retail tax will only increase the expenditure for government services through welfare systems, rather than raise revenue amounts from the Retail tax. Other tax systems must be devised, to raise the revenues to pay for government services; all effective tax assessments will shift the tax burden from the Consumer under such conditions.

The Retail percentage tax probably serves as excellent vehicle to propel Stagflation, as was seen in the 1980s. Investment schedules vastly rise without addition to Consumption, so Capital return ratios drop drastically. Basic Consumption-recovery mechanisms—Product Sales—are curtailed by the tax assessment, so Unemployment continues to rise. The income of households start to split, with households under employment gaining income faster than their rate of Consumption; due to the cost of Consumption. Households without employment quickly drop to poverty levels.

The Author would like to point out at this point, all tax systems discussed concern the same relevant withdrawal of tax amounts to pay for government services. The manner of how and where they are withdrawn, vitally effects the health of the Economy. It is not a question of whether the revenues need to be withdrawn; government services must be financed in some method. The accumulation of government debt may be the most ineffective of all forms of finance, in the economic sense.

Government debt has been aggregating for decades, with few short years of budget surplus. A real test of Government debt viability lies in the debt service. Years of budget surplus repaid Government debt at a much slower rate, than was the rate of debt gain in years of deficit. The number of years of deficit vastly exceed the years of surplus. Government economic policy still adheres to Keynesian ideas of deficit spending to fuel the Economy. The Government does this by tax reductions, which they do not intend to repay in good economic times.

The above scenario generates curses among some Economists, who know the Federal debt could have been paid off in the 1990s with adequate taxation; without curtailing the economic growth of the Period. This would have required suppression of Government spending, of the order of Pork barrel; and maintenance of taxation of profits. Holding

Government salaries of all employees—elected, nominated, and employed—to the rate of inflation during the 1990s, would have saved Government expenditures at least 10 Billion dollars alone per year; or approximately 100 Billion dollars. Delay of funding of any Enactment between 1990 and 2002 for one calender year past passage, would have saved the American Taxpayer some 300 Billion dollars of expenditure; any American Taxpayer can ask why We need such expenditure this year, if We did not have it last year. Delay of a decade could have saved 2.5 Trillion dollars.

Return to the Retail tax indicates it, like the Wholesale tax, stands as a very bad tax system. Government excess spending holds enough damage for the American economy, without implanting taxes which actually harm the functioning of the Economy. Tax systems, once implemented, develop a life of their own; becoming almost impossible to get rid of, as all generate their own political support. The tax collectors hired to service the tax system, alone provide an intense lobby for the continuance of the tax system. The American Taxpayer needs no further injury, and should adamantly oppose new tax ideas; where the gains and benefits are not fully examined.

18

The Capital Tax

This tax exhibits a robust nature which the Author enjoys, though he is almost alone among Economists. The nature of the tax is simple: each Taxpayer subtracts his liabilities from his Assets, and pays an assessment upon the difference; the assessment generally quoted along like lines with Sales tax rates. There is no question such a tax would generate adequate revenues, under proper percentage rates. Now it is time to air the misgivings of Economists.

The general Economic argument states a Capital tax demands a uniform rate of Capital return for viability. Capital returns vary not only by Capital usage, but by economic sector of investment. Any Capital tax would make some economic sectors less viable than competitive sectors; under the condition of search for investment funds. The impact of a Capital tax would distort market allocation of resources and labor.

Answer to the general Economic argument asserts market allocation is a continuous process, constantly integrating new Cost factors into the price structure of the market. The market distortion of market allocation could be beneficial, rather than harmful to the Economy; especially if such allocation also entailed reduction of adverse tax costing elsewhere. The Capital tax would be the most direct tax assessing the advantage any economic unit gains under the market system. It would mean the greatest beneficiaries of the economy paid the greatest share, and so is the fairest, progressive tax.

Specific Economic argument against the Capital tax claims this tax would lead all participants in the economy to engage in excessive accumulation of debt; all in an attempt to nullify the tax impact. It further claims any deduction limitation on the accumulation of debt, to forestall debt tax evasion; would adversely impact the capitalization of enterprise. Excessive debt service levels would suborn any viable tax revenues from the Capital tax, without resolution to the loss.

Counter-argument to the above analysis comes with statement a Debt charge could be instituted to Debt accumulation above a certain level of assets. Individual could be given tax freedom below $50,000 worth of debt, and Business given tax freedom below $250,000 worth of debt; but all are charged a debt fee equal to the Interest rate on the debt, above these amounts. This would make the debt charge tax equivalent to twice the Capital tax assessment, and work to reduction of debt with the accumulation of Wealth.

The Capital tax with accompanying debt service tax provides advantage to new households and young Workers, allowing them to accumulate Assets faster; due to an absence of abusive tax. The tax would mainly impact established households and higher incomes, who have the ability to pay, plus the ability to fund their entrepreneurial efforts. Reductions of other forms of tax could actually provide these individuals and households with less exertion of payment.

The market allocation argument basically concerns capitalization of enterprise. Absolutely free market allocation provides for variations of Capital returns, which are economically unviable for maintaining a stable Money Supply; which necessitates a relatively stable Capital return base, without extreme variations. Introduction of a Capital tax could provide Capital return stability, by reallocating resources in a manner where product supply is subject to more uniform costs. Labor would shift between Sectors, and product supply reductions would raise unit prices; all providing greater conformity to overall market values.

A major economic contribution which the Capital tax may provide could be a more uniform capitalization of sector enterprises. Many sectors of production lag in technological advance capitalization, because of current rates of Capital return; of sufficient largesse to nullify incentive for upgrading. A Capital tax would insist they maintain the same economic performance factors as other sectors, especially concerning hourly output, and unit production costs. The Capital tax would tie these under-capitalized sectors more tightly in economic performance, to the overall economy.

An important element of the Capital tax resides in the pressure to utilize property, or sell it. The constant charge for retention propels productive use of capital possession. This becomes vital in the context of abandoned property, a major source of economic loss to this Country. The tax stops current practice of operating facilities until they become obsolete, then letting them be taken for back property taxes; a practice widely practiced by both business and individuals. The Capital tax would force ownership to update the property, sell it for whatever price attainable, or start legal action to transfer by Sheriff's Sale. The tax requires active registry of all property.

Tax Evasion of such a Capital tax would be no easier than evading Personal Income tax, and the tax agency construct could maintain similar Accounting procedures. Proper wording of the enacting legislation would eliminate all exemptions under the current Income tax law, so the volume would be vastly increased; as Social Security recipients and Welfare cases would also be evaluated for tax. Business would find no immunity of any type, while Government Bond holdings of all types will be included in evaluation of total Assets. Utilities, especially Power companies, would find themselves taxed; negating years of lobbying to reduce business taxes. The size of tax supervisory personnel would likely double, though tax evasion has little chance of success.

The cost of tax collection vastly increase under the Capital tax, due to the widespread nature of reportage of Assets. Tax Checks of Returns evolve negotiating arrangements with foreign banks to report holdings of American citizens and companies. Legislation need be enacted forcing registry of businesses as American companies, when their volume of

American trade exceeds certain limits; the probable evaluation may be ten million dollars worth of Sales to American customers per year. All of these intricate reportage arrangements potentially triple the cost of tax collections as now exist under the Income tax system.

The expected revenue increase would be substantial, because of the wider inclusion of taxable elements. Readers need understand the alteration in placement of tax: the Capital tax does not tax performance, but possession; while the Income tax only taxes economic performance. The nature of the tax penalizes poor economic performance, inflicting greatest tax impact upon those who are current economic failures. This impels transfer of Assets to those who can most efficiently perform with those assets, while failures in the economic sector must transfer to financial instruments; whose profitability resides under the control of others. This becomes one of the most beneficial of the residual advantages of the Capital tax.

The actual tax revenue amounts can only be judged with the consideration of the percentage rate imposed by a Capital tax. Many Economists would suggest a percentage rate approximate to provision of revenue amounts equivalent to the current Income tax system. The Author would adamantly disagree. A change of the form of taxation should provide for a viable economic alteration to the proliferation of taxing systems now present. A unified tax system will be more economical for Government expenditure, and eventually less costly to the Taxpayers.

The substitution of the Capital tax should include elimination of Personal Income tax, Business taxes, Corporate Income taxes, Capital Gains taxes, Property taxes, Sales taxes, and most Excise taxes. This should be done in a framework for a balanced budget and repayment of all current Government debt, at all levels of Government. This would probably call for a specific Constitutional amendment clearly outlining and dictating revenue sharing between the three levels of Government; based upon percentage evaluation of Government level expenditures.

Such an integrated plan of taxation would call for Veto power shared by all three levels of Government, to limit any excessive expenditures by any one level. A standing Conference Committee on Taxation need be established, with representation from all three levels of Government. The Committee to resolve issues of revenue dispersion and the percentage rate of taxation, based upon the current needs of Government; debt aggregation determined by passage by the representative bodies of all three levels. This involved process defeats a potential uniform system of taxation, as it faces deep political objections at all levels of Government.

The total complexity of Capital tax reportage, though, nullifies most advantages of the Capital tax, unless it can be implemented as a uniform tax system; eliminating exterior forms of taxation. The cost of maintaining the tax system makes it inefficient, if it only replaces the current Income tax system; the cost of collection would triple to attain the same level of tax revenue. The real value to the Capital tax system would be the elimination of the Property tax, Sales tax, and Income tax systems, a process crossing the three levels of Government. Legislative bodies at all three levels will oppose this loss of power to tax.

19
The Education Tax

The current form of Education provision in the United States stands as an abomination. This is not to detract from the quality of this Education, which is high and accelerating. The horror resides within the forms of financing the Education. Basic Education receives funding from Property taxes, with assistance grants from States and Federal allotments. This only concerns the basic procedures of paying for books, materials, teacher salaries, and utility costs. The basic Construction costs of Primary and Secondary education must be funded by issuance of Bonds, with State and Federal grants. Any major School Board in this Country could have up to thirty sources of revenue to fund primary and secondary education, approximately half must eventually be repaid; through some exercise of Property taxation, or debt rollover to State or Federal agency. Property tax allotments are normally insufficient to fund normal education expenses, with debt service cutting into operational funds already lacking.

Higher Education functions in even worse straits than basic Education. State provision of funds hardly extends beyond the provision of physical plant, with Students expected to pay for normal operating costs of collegiate and specialized education. The Federal Government provides Research grants to Universities, and loans and grants to Students; all in hopes that costs will not continue to escalate. Parents and Students go into debt slavery to pay tuition, while scholarships grow exponentially as tax laws cooperate (an estimated fifty thousand new ones per year). The average College graduate can expect to owe at least two years' salary, by the time he finally graduates and get his first professional job.

The Community College network presents the sole bright light in the entire spectrum of education, providing basic vocational skills; at prices which Students and Business can almost afford. The spectacular effect of this education exists in the fact a Student can expect some sort of income within a reasonable time. The quality of education also attains a high standard, as a majority of courses are taught by personnel with prior field experience of length. Community colleges give a well-taught limited education for a reasonable price. States maintain the majority of Construction and utilities expense, with Federal assistance.

The proper taxation for funding of Education must await alteration in educational practice, for several reasons; not the least, limitations placed on charges to Student as tuition. Federal legislation should be enacted, stipulating effective limits of tuition charges, based upon standard Wage scales for Instructors, Administration, and Maintenance. A proposal would state all educational institutions can charge no more than 25% for maintenance of plant, 25% for administrative costs, and 50% for Instructors and instructional aids. These charges are to be based upon IRS-established Means for Wage scales in the Educational sector, including Community Colleges and State Universities. A proportion of the law establishing such limits should assert enrollment must be based solely on academic attainment, or meeting State standards for admission.

Such a law would not limit the extent of Salary paid to any in the Educational sector, or limit the growth of maintenance or administrative employment. The law does insist extraordinary growth in such Costs, as well as marked Instructor salaries; cannot be shifted to the Student, or his Parents. The Reader need understand such excess Costs have nothing to do with the quality of education received, and benefits only the infrastructure of the educational institution. Student and Parent are expected to feed the desires for large staffs and high salaries.

Study of the educational function highlights the real fact Education rarely benefits the Community directly. Charging elements of the Community for the cost of educating students, when such education only effectively provides profits for future generations; is idiocy, especially as most educated earn such profits elsewhere than where raised. Sixty percent of the tax base charged for this education possess either stable incomes, or reduced incomes from retirement or disability. Addition of skilled labor to the Labor Supply means absolutely nothing to these individuals in economic terms. They are taxed unfairly for a service which they did not receive themselves, or so long before, their contribution has already been paid repetitively.

The only real beneficiaries of education reduce to Employers and Employees. Employers gain because of the supply of skilled labor cadres. Employees gain from higher Wage payments for extended Education. Parents do not even gain from the better positioning of their children, as only two percent of children provide remuneration to their Parents; most of this remuneration being paid as minimal support payments of no great magnitude. Tax placement for Education remains completely misplaced, with real tax evasion from the beneficiaries of education.

Employers and Employees should each be taxed for every labor hour worked, as automatic charge for employment. The tax placed upon Employers should go immediately to the local Education district, funding basic education; the magnitude of the charge should fund basic education totally. Federal law should regulate this magnitude of tax to the Employer, and mandate shift of revenues from locales of high employment, to sectors of low employment. The magnitude of this shift must be constrained to the Mean cost of Students in the basic education program times the numbers of Students in the locale. This law does not assure equality of educational opportunity, only the same monetary assistance per Student.

A most essential element to such an Educational tax must be the prohibition of basic education facilities from abnormal debt service for educational purposes; best constrained by prohibition of debt extension past five years of expected revenues. School districts of low Student population will have to use Consolidated schools with other districts, in order to obtain equality of educational opportunity for Students. The Federal law must be adamant in statement Employer Tax will be the sole source of revenue for basic education, with no other taxes or assessments assigned to Taxpayers.

Higher education payment will be altered to be paid by Social Security taxation. Students qualifying for extended education (relatively easy through all educational facilities) will receive a tuition payment equal to the amount charged, but not to exceed the Mean charge of tuition by State Universities. The Student is also to receive a stipend for books and life maintenance not larger than the sum of a 40-hour Minimum wage Workweek, for each week of attendance (Instructors must fill out mandated attendance charts). The total sum is to be paid monthly, so as to not alter the Social Security payments schedules. Students will be allowed to work outside of their academic attendance as they wish, but they will have to maintain a full academic schedule for full-time Students.

Social Security will set up negative balance accounts for these Students, who will have to pay for their own education; as excess Social Security tax assessments, scaled over a twenty year period. The empowering legislation for the Education tax will mandate Educational institutions must accept such Students up to forty percent of their Student body, if the Students can meet academic standards for attendance; with tuition payment limited to the Social Security allotment for tuition; otherwise, these educational institutions will lose all tax-financed aid, assistance, or grants.

Economic analysis of such a Educational tax suggests Employer and Employee could treat such taxation as normal operating costs, which have insufficient magnitude to affect economic performance. The imposition of this tax would free local Communities of the heavy burden of maintaining quality education for Students, and free Taxpayers of tax burden which actually detracts from their lifestyle. Students may estimate they will receive a greater uniformity in quality of education, plus greater freedom of access to education opportunity. Graduates of educational systems will not be burdened by excess debt, in the midst of establishment of new households.

Overall economic benefit states Business will be enabled in scheduling operating costs, where a variable has turned into a relative constant. The Economy will enjoy a highly-skilled Labor force adequately funded; the overall effect more beneficial than the G.I. Bill after WWII. Educational facilities will be assured of a constancy of funding, without resort to public votes on Bond issuance. Taxpayers will gain from the unification of funding for a heavy public expense; with an estimated reduction of total taxation by at least three percent. Debt Service charges for Education should reduce by at least one-quarter of the current magnitude—an immense savings from total taxation.

20

Specialized Excise Taxes.

Excise taxes remain a fun vehicle for gathering Governmental revenue, because they are taxes charged upon use of a product or service. The Consumer can regulate his payment of the tax, if it is known; by his degree of usage of the product or service. Effective imposition of the Excise leaves the Consumer unconcerned about the tax payment, because it makes only a marginal element of the cost of product or service. Improper use of Excise attempts to tax adjudged bad behavior—like the Sin taxes. All generate revenue, some extremely large amounts of Government funding.

The greatest problem with Excise taxes come from lack of uniformity of placement, which makes accounting difficult for both business and taxing agent; and for lack of legislative overview of the placement of such Excises. Legislators forget the previous placement of such Excises in many cases, and return for further placement; finding they can only increase an excise, not impose a new one. This causes the products under excise to multiply in number with greater tax impact, while study of economic effects of tax impact is lost. Taxing agents soon deal with an extreme range of products excised, all with different tax amounts; difficult to administrate, hard to even inform business of the various excises charged.

Overview of Excise taxation gives insight into the process. Excises should be imposed on ranges of general products, all of uniform size; a Can of Beans should have the same excise as any other Can of anything. A large Can should have the same excise, as a small Can. Confusion and inadvertent tax evasion spread with variations of excise. Multiplicity of products generate the same confusion.

General Class Excises should be imposed for garnering revenue, specialized Excises imposed only to generate economic factor change. This Work already explored the use of a specialized Excise on Beef steak, to alter the economic performance in the supply of overall Beef. Such use of specialized Excise cannot work effectively, in the face of multiplicity of excised products. The economic generative effects of the Excise used, are nullified by the counteractive effects of other excises. General Class Excises, though, do not distract from the placement of specialized excises for economic effect.

The difference between the two types of Excises can be best explained by suggested placement of General Excise taxes to generate revenue. The Author will utilize what General Excises he believes should be imposed on the American economy, for the simple purpose of raising government revenue to provide ability to eliminate alternative present taxation. The Reader should study the following carefully, as the Author will try to express the benefits of tax substitution as well.

The Author believes a Eatery Excise tax should be imposed, magnitude of five cents; payable each and every time the Cash Register is used in all Restaurants, Bars, Coffee houses, and Refreshment stands. Most say this would be a horrible tax, but almost All would not notice the tax at all. The Author would also state Consumer use of these establishments is of such frequency, the Property tax nationwide could potentially be cut in half. Would Anyone notice the increase in Cost for service? Would Anyone notice a Property tax reduction of such size?

He also likes the thought of a Entertainment Excise as well, at the cost of fifty cents per ticket, for entrance to Clubs, Sporting Events, Concerts, Roller rinks, Cinemas, and Personal Appearance events. Americans are addicted to large-scale group events for Entertainment, this affinity will not be diminished by imposition of an Excise tax. The low cost of the Excise would not impact Consumption of these services, even at the level of grade school plays and middle school football games. The Author wishes he could place such excise upon Church attendance, to really propel generation of revenue. The financial generation of such an Excise would be immense, even without the Constitutional Conflict question; and such a tax, would find far greater ease of payment than other forms.

High School Sports contests would generate a probable average of $300 per event, the average Little League game gains an average $50 per event. Professional Football games would generate about $30,000 per game, with Pro Baseball bringing about a equivalent amount. Professional Basketball and Soccer games could be estimated to bring in $3000–5000 per game. Golf Tournaments would likely bring in $5000 per day of competition, with Tennis matches bringing in half that amount. Movie houses could average up to $500,000 per night, on a Nationwide basis. Concerts average an attendance of 6000, so excise revenues of $3000 per performance. TV audiences for taping Shows would bring around $200 per show. Amusement Parks might average $150,000 per day, year-round. Would attendance drop at these Group entertainments? Highly unlikely. The attendance at National and State Parks would generate $400,000 per day, without drop of attendance.

The above cited Excises would generate immense revenue, with relatively no drop in usage of such services. The Revenues gained could potentially cut all other forms of taxation by as much as one-quarter. The Tax impact of the General Excise taxes would be minor, only calling for slight expansion of entertainment allowance per household; estimated at $300 per household, spread over yearly usage. This is much easier tax payment than lump-sum tax payments which must be budgeted. The expansion of entertainment allowances do not alter budgeting for necessities from household income, as do almost all other forms of taxation. The current Economic argument against Excise taxation need be revisited.

Turn to discussion of specialized Excise taxes brings much heat to Economic argument. Almost half of all Economists deny judicious exercise of specialized excise has any effect on production cost accounting. They claim such excise is treated as simple taxation, and passed in total to the Consumer; who is faced with an unrelenting market price, so Consumer preferences remain the same. They assert as this is the case, use of Excise taxation to regulate economic performance is basically valueless. They go on to state such taxation does not even raise revenues, as the specialization of tax procedures and supervision costs cancel almost all expected gains. Consumer Demand will normalize after a short intermediate period, and no effect is noted; except for a loss of Consumption, due to the waste of Consumer dollars.

Economists who favor Excise, including the Author, assert business does respond rapidly to diminishment of product consumption in the short-run, do reallocate supply schedules to alternate product supply, and do adjust their long-term price schedule; in attempts to maximize Sales of the excised product. They continue to state most of the extraordinary tax collection expense diminish as excise payment becomes standard business procedure, and eventual tax collections will reach levels half of the Consumer payment. They contend the flexibility of business supply and price schedules do make excises a primary instrument for Government economic policy implementation, in the area of regulating Consumer Demand among products; all in the effort to maximize total economic performance.

Suggesting Excise taxes to be placed can be Economic suicide, as well as political suicide. This caused by the wide inter-flux of economic impacts possible. Extraneous economic influences may intrude, which had not even been considered before placement of the excise. A calculated impact may have the total opposite effect, because of outside factors; i.e., foreign purchase might increase to cancel domestic reductions of purchase, a rise in resource cost might triple the impact of the excise, such tax might generate alteration of transport used, or new technological product might destroy the viability of the product with addition of excise. Legislative action tends to lack flexibility, and Excises of adverse effect; should be removed rapidly. The above considerations contain much material for criticism of Excise as form of economic regulation. The above 'dodging the bullet' justification can now be put aside, and the Author will enter into discussion of viable specialized Excise taxes. He uses excesses in the American economy as excuse for the imposition of excise in the beginning cases. American income levels are affluent for over half of the American households. This affluence leads to over-Consumption of a wide variety of products, both for entertainment and for personal image. Business personnel travel almost three times as much as they need, for the simple reason they express a generous expense account. One-half of American households take 6.5 days more Vacation time, than do other households around the World—the average yearly Vacation time remaining about ten days. Current tax regulation incites almost 37% more Advertising, than most Economic studies indicate provide saturation. Almost seventy percent of all Air cargo would be more economically transported by alternate transportation. All of the above could be impacted by proper placement of Excise taxes.

A Transportation Ticket Excise Tax could be placed, to slow the temporary migration patterns of the American people; this style of travel clogs Airports, highways, and flight patterns. The effect of Terrorism did not effectively alter the existence of over-capitalized Airlines, and crowded Airspace and highway. The above cited Excise should be set to capitalize necessary transportation facilities: so Bus Tickets would have excise of $2, Train tickets excise of $10, and Airline tickets would be charge excise of $30. Fuel Station Excise would be $1 per use of the gas pump; whether you use it to fill a gallon can for the lawnmower, or fill a Tractor-trailer. The revenue from such taxes would be large, and inhibit travel which was unnecessary.

An Advertisement Excise Tax will reduce the use of Advertising above necessary limit. The Excise Tax for placement of Ad-space in a Newspaper, Magazine, or other form of Periodical will be eight cents per column line; larger Business ads will be charged by use of effective column lines. Postal Excise will charge $3 per lb. of total shipped material; this is over and above Postal rates. These Excise taxes can be expected to reduce Business advertisement by about forty percent, saving Paper and Printing costs; with a residual three percent reduction in overall product prices. They will also reduce pressure on Postal services, and contract the need for added Landfill space by almost six percent.

The imposition of a $1 per parcel charge for all Air freight will reduce total freight shipped by Air an estimated 23%. This will greatly refund railway and trucking, and not functionally slow business production. Economic studies have indicated it may increase Warehouse costs by around nine percent. Many businesses work directly on use of Air cargo for transport, because of ease of distribution and speed. There are alternatives for them.

The Author advocates passage of legislation to alter Postal service, where bulk shipments can be sent to specific Post Offices; where Postal employees will be entailed to break them open, and deliver the piecemeal franked packages. Advertisements specifically could not be shipped in this manner—only products and catalogues. Private shipping like FEDEX and UPS will follow suit almost immediately, and business which depends upon overnight deliveries can survive. The majority of business, though, will revert to slower delivery times, with cheaper transportation costs.

Study of the above recommendations express some of these Excises conflict with each other; the Fuel Station Excise cancels impact of the Excise on Air cargo for example. The placement of all these excises, though, will have long-term economic impact; altering and adjusting the methodology of business to maximize profits in their usage of such services. There will be curtailment of unnecessary travel, and there will be appropriate use of transport facilities. The revenues generated by specialized Excise taxes can be devoted to improvements in the affected industries, like to pay for the change in Postal shipping arrangements.

General Excise taxation can be used to substitute for alternate tax systems which possess adverse effects.

21

Conclusion.

Two views of taxation live among Economists: one view contends Taxes are a basic good, the other view see Taxes as a pestilence which wastes natural economic incentives. The first group of Economists know government services have to be funded, these government services provide more economic incentive than it destroys, and believe adequate placement of taxation can bring added economic incentive and benefit. The other group witnesses only reductions of capital accumulation, reductions of Labor and Entrepreneurial incentives, wastage of economic resources towards welfare services, and lowered economic performance from loss of income for Taxpayers. Neither side will ever win, because it is basically a Mind-set; approving or disapproving of Government.

Business could not survive with the action of Government; which validates Contracts, provides a skilled Labor force, and maintains a Money Supply and financial institutions. Government grants right of debt abrogation through Bankruptcy law, and guarantees provision of advertised product. All Businessmen, and one group of Economists, think this is natural rights; forgetting the centuries of effect to attain the fairness of the present system. They perceive all Government provision of services which do not directly benefit themselves, remains in the realm of unnecessary expense and over-extension of government; especially if it costs themselves any taxation. It is not as selfish as it seems;

the Author finds Government to be over-large, too intrusive of most aspects of American life, and costing too much.

What these businessmen and one group of Economists fail to understand, consists of the nature of Government. Half the cost of Government could not be reduced without increased production costs for Business; who would lack trained labor, adequate communication and transportation facilities, and protection from theft and fraud. Charges for financial transfers would be at least five times as high as present, with greater insecurity. Work safety regulations (the whole complex of regulations concerning Work, Consumer Protection, Road safety, and security of communications and transfers) save business approximately one-quarter of total production costs, if such security had to be privately supplied. Such Government protection must be awarded to all.

The hated welfare transfers so often touted as outrageous burden by way of taxation, brings business approximately twenty percent of Consumption of product and service which they supply. This comes from welfare recipients, Government workers, and Government supply contracts. Persistent desire to fund Government services by expansion of public debt, rather than taxation; actively curtails the amount of future Consumption, and reduces future Profits. Provision of welfare transfer payments expands future Consumption and Profits, as numerous economic studies indicate.

Those Economists who favor taxation, see the process operating to curtail the extremity of economic incentives; which unrestrained markets allow. Cancellation of monopolies expands production, and cuts Consumer costs; which allows for greater production under the same matrix of resources. Progressive taxation has been proven by economic studies to raise the overall standard of living, by imposing greater taxation on those with the ability to pay. The important element to remember for the Student of Economics: a Progressive tax base leads to an increasing Middle Class as proportion of total numbers, a Regressive tax base finds elements of the Middle Class following to lower classes faster than entrance to the Middle Class. Tax equals the playing field more effectively, than any other form of regulation.

Taxation can actually expand economic performance, as Government funds Research and Development of economic components, which are too expensive for Private Sector investment; due to the risks involved, or the delayed Profits payment. River flow projects would not have been implemented, and flooding would still be a greater problem than it now is. Rural electrification would not have taken place, nor would there be an Interstate system; as States and Business could not fund either alone. Government is a major landowner, who is also one of the greatest Developers existent; Government constructions alone have provided a third of the Profits to the Construction industry, over the last Century. The comment Government is bad for business is not only a lie, but shows the idiocy of the Speaker.

Taxes can be used to suppress consumption of undesired Goods, impel consumption of favored Goods, and create higher production of Goods through taxation of Substitute products. They have the facility of equalizing Incomes, and thereby; standardizing Consumption patterns for greater Profitability at a higher standard of living. They are a fluid medium for gathering government revenues to provide for services, without heavy elements of extortion. Taxes can even further production when properly used, because they induce greater production efforts to maintain total Profitability from marginal Profits off unit production.

The entire Economic argument concerning proper Public debt levels retains the air of morbidity. The Author believes Public debt levels should not exceed those necessary to amortize Government constructions—which are paid off future taxation. Resistance to taxation comes only from felt tax impact by Taxpayers, and is totally the fault of Legislators; who do not understand principles of Tax spread to defray tax impact. The Author feels no Government, even under recessive economic conditions, should be unable to maintain itself free of Public debt. A proper assortment of tax systems, of limited impact, could generate sufficient revenue. Economic principles for fueling the Economy through deficit spending are a Cop-out, which never operate on the root causes for Recessions.

Economic recessions result from economic imbalances, these caused by unequal rates of growth between economic sectors. These economic imbalances are not addressed by the removal of taxes, or reduced percentage taxation. They are addressed by the imposition of taxes in the correct location, to provide incentive to slower sectors, and retard more successful sectors. Further Government efforts under recessive conditions should contain measures of Public sector employment and supply/construction contracts, all designed not to provide relief for the Poor; but to raise the Consumption pattern of those employed, through high wages. This is the cure for Recession, as the Author sees it.

Taxes will always be with Us. We can use different tax forms to better economic condition, or We can ruin economic incentives by destructive tax impact. Government services must be paid for, the method of payment being 'Pay as We go'; public debt service only magnifies tax impact, it does not reduce it. Dedication to ideology when considering taxation remains the worst determination for tax placement. Several considerations must be observed in the placement of taxes: Taxpayers must have the ability to pay, Business must make normal production profits, and Consumers must retain Discretionary funds. Anything else will lead to disaster, both to Government and Economy.

0-595-25795-X